simple pleasures

simple pleasures

edible gifts for friends & family

Stephanie Evans,
Andrew Franks & Susanna Tee

APPLE

First published in the UK in 2008 by
Apple Press
7 Greenland Street
London NW1 0ND
United Kingdom
www.apple-press.com

ISBN 978 1 84543 293 5

This book was conceived, designed and produced by
Ivy Press
The Old Candlemakers
West Street
Lewes, East Sussex
BN7 2NZ, UK
www.ivy-group.co.uk

Creative Director Peter Bridgewater
Publisher Jason Hook
Editorial Director Caroline Earle
Art Director Clare Harris
Senior Editor Lorraine Turner
Designer Mike Morey
Photographer Jeremy Hopley
Home Economists Hélène Adamczewski, Rosie Hopper
Illustrator John Woodcock
Concept Design Wayne Blades
Packaging Design Michelle Tilly

Printed and bound in China.

1 3 5 7 9 10 8 6 4 2

Author contributions by page number:
Stephanie Evans 42–77
Andrew Franks 8–41, 110–141
Susanna Tee 78–109

contents

Introduction

If the nicest and most personal gifts are those that you've made yourself, then perhaps the best of all are those that can be opened and shared between host and guest – the freshly baked cake that can be sliced and served straight away, the home-brewed liqueur that can be uncorked and poured into glasses around the table, the chutney that can be served to accompany the meal. These gifts are not difficult or time-consuming to make, and do not need hours of harried time in the kitchen. *Simple Pleasures* helps you to rediscover the easy, edible gifts that are part of the visitor's tradition: simple strawberry jam and quince jelly; almond cakes and sumptuous brownies for a welcome teatime call, and homemade limoncello or elderflower cordial in pretty bottles, ready to hand over and be served straight away. These recipes aren't complex, but straightforward and elegant; most are speedy and all are delicious and can be enjoyed as part of any easygoing visit or a meal with friends.

Some are also accompanied by suggestions for ways in which you can wrap or present them. Again, these are simple – and of course you can ignore them if you prefer: a beautiful cake will be as welcome in a plain container as it will be in a decorative box. If you want to complete the picture, though (and this is often as much for the giver's satisfaction as it is for that of the recipient), then you should go ahead, safe in the knowledge that even the most elaborate of presentations won't take more than half-an-hour or so of your time, and that these extra touches will be more in the nature of finishing flourishes than fussy or over-anxious extras. You'll find that your homemade treats attract admiration out of all proportion to the effort they've taken to make. You may even decide that some of them are so easy that they become part of your own repertoire at home, too.

Jams, Preserves & Chutneys

Jams, preserves and chutneys make some of the prettiest food presents. Their jewel-like colours look enticing even in the plainest glass jar, and they are surprisingly easy and quick to make. Even if you are a jam novice, you'll be able to manage all the recipes in this chapter. Before you start though, do read through to the end any recipes you're considering: some of them call for overnight draining, steeping or soaking, and although none of these processes requires any effort from you, the maker, the time still needs to be factored into your calculations.

Lemon curd

This tastes wonderfully fresh and sharp, yet will keep for two months after it is opened provided that it is kept refrigerated. It is a versatile gift, useful for everything from a delicious spread for toast to a fragrant filling for homemade cakes and tarts. It's a real from-one-cook-to-another present. When you've mastered the lemon version, try some of the more unusual variations opposite. For an elegant gift (but slightly more hard work), you could give jars of three different flavours – passion fruit, strawberry and lemon – in one lavish box. The different pastels – pink, orange and yellow – look beautiful together. You can double or treble the quantities, as long as you have a saucepan/bowl combination or double boiler that is large enough.

Makes: two 350g *(12oz)* jars

Preparation time: 10 minutes

Cooking time: about 40 minutes

Ingredients

4 lemons

450g *(1lb)* granulated sugar

225g *(8oz)* unsalted butter

Method

1 Zest all four lemons and squeeze the juice of three of them. Put the juice and zest into a large, heatproof bowl together with the sugar and butter.

2 Place the bowl over a saucepan of simmering water. The steam should heat the base of the bowl but the bowl should not touch the water.

3 Stir the mixture over a low heat until the ingredients have melted together. Once the mixture has melted, it will take a further 20–30 minutes of cooking before the mixture thickens sufficiently to set. Keep stirring and scraping down the sides of the bowl constantly.

4 After the curd has been cooking for 20 minutes, drop a teaspoonful on a cold saucer and leave it to cool for a minute. When cool, the mixture should be the consistency of thick yogurt. If it is still too runny, cook for another 5–10 minutes, stirring constantly.

5 When a spoonful of curd sets like thick yogurt on the saucer, carefully decant the mixture into clean, sterilized jars, then seal and label. Unopened, the curd will keep for a year; after opening, you should keep the jar in the refrigerator and use it within two months.

Variations

Strawberry curd

To make strawberry curd, replace the
lemon juice with 450g *(1lb)* of hulled ripe
strawberries. Liquidize them briefly in a
blender, then sieve the resulting purée
to get rid of the pips. Melt the sugar and
butter in a heatproof bowl set over a
saucepan of simmering water, then add
the strawberries and proceed with the
rest of the recipe in the same way as for
lemon curd.

Passion fruit curd

To make passion fruit curd, replace the
lemon juice with the pulp from six ripe
passion fruit. You can sieve it if you prefer,
but many cooks think that the curd tastes
better with the slightly sour crunch of
the seeds left in. As with the strawberry
curd, let the butter and sugar melt and mix
together before adding the passion fruit
pulp. Then proceed with the rest of the
recipe in the same way as for lemon curd.

Strawberry jam

Of all the jams you can make, strawberry is the most different from commercial versions, with a delicate, true strawberry taste that never seems to carry through to even the most expensive branded variety. Make this in summer using ripe strawberries to get the true flavour – don't use the imported, perpetually underripe strawberries you can buy year-round in every supermarket. The two challenges of strawberry jam are, first, to keep the berries whole in the jam and stop them from disintegrating, and, second, to get them evenly distributed through the jars. Follow this recipe carefully and you should be able to achieve both goals!

Makes: two 500g *(1lb 2oz)* jars

Preparation time: 20 minutes, plus overnight maceration

Cooking time: about 15–20 minutes

Ingredients

1.8kg *(4lb)* fresh strawberries
(they should be ripe but not over-ripe)
1.8kg *(4lb)* jam sugar
2 lemons

Method

1 Start the night before you want to cook your jam. Place the strawberries in a large bowl and cover them carefully with the jam sugar (unlike ordinary sugar, jam sugar contains pectin, which helps the jam to set).

2 The following day, carefully decant the sugar and the strawberries into a large saucepan or preserving pan. Squeeze the lemons and add their juice to the mixture.

3 Place the pan over a low heat and cook slowly, to allow the sugar to dissolve. Stir frequently, but gently, turning over the fruit and sugar rather than crushing them together (this is easier to do with a heatproof spatula than with a spoon).

4 When the sugar has dissolved, increase the heat and bring the jam to the boil. Cook at a rolling boil for 3 minutes, then remove the pan from the heat and drop a teaspoonful onto a saucer and allow it to cool for a minute. If it sets, the jam is ready; if it remains liquid, return the pan to the heat and boil for another 2 minutes and test again. As soon as you have a 'set', take the pan off the heat.

5 Use a shallow spoon to skim any scum from the surface of the jam, then leave it to cool in the pan for 10 minutes (this short wait will help the strawberries to distribute evenly through the jam when potted). Then carefully ladle the jam into warm, sterilized jars. Unopened, this jam should keep for a year. Once opened, you should keep the jar in the refrigerator and use within two months.

Mint jelly

Although mint jelly is the traditional partner for cold lamb (much as mint sauce accompanies hot lamb), it goes well with any cold meats, and is great in a sandwich. Do not be put off by the rather small amount of mint in this recipe – the flavour infuses the apple-based jelly, and even people who didn't think they liked mint will find its delicacy appealing. It looks prettiest in small jelly jars. Use ordinary garden mint, rather than any of the fashionable scented varieties such as pineapple or orange-scented mint; it works better.

Makes: five 175g *(6oz)* jars

Preparation time: 10 minutes, plus 4 hours or overnight to strain

Cooking time: about 30 minutes

Ingredients

3 lemons
1.8kg *(4lb)* cooking apples, washed
1.4 litres *(2½ pints)* water
1 heaped tbsp chopped fresh garden mint leaves, plus 10 fresh sprigs
granulated sugar, 450g *(1lb)* for each 600ml *(1 pint)* of juice

Method

1 Squeeze the lemons and save the juice. Roughly chop the apples – don't peel them – and put them into a large preserving pan together with the water, the lemon juice and five sprigs of the fresh mint.

2 Cook the apples until they are soft and fluffy, then pour the mixture into a muslin jelly bag if you have one (a clean tea towel is fine if you don't), support it over a bowl and leave it for at least 4 hours, or overnight. Do not be tempted to squeeze the mixture through the bag because this will lead to a cloudy jelly.

3 Measure the apple juice into a preserving pan, and for every 600ml *(1 pint)* of juice add 450g *(1lb)* of granulated sugar. Add the remaining mint sprigs and slowly bring the mixture to the boil.

4 Boil rapidly until a teaspoonful dropped onto a saucer sets after a minute or two – you may need to boil the jelly for 15–20 minutes until it reaches setting point. Then remove the mint sprigs and skim off any scum that has formed on the surface and allow the jelly to cool for 5 minutes before mixing in the chopped mint.

5 Ladle the jelly into small, warm, sterilized jars, then seal and label. Unopened, this jelly will keep for a year. Once opened, you should keep the jar in the refrigerator and use within two months.

East India chutney

This is a very old recipe, and no-one seems quite sure how it got its name, although the range of dried fruits and spices it contains may have seemed exotic to the early cook – or, of course, it may actually have come from East India. It makes a rich, thick and luscious chutney with a tangy flavour that works well with hearty meats and cheeses (it's perfect with a ploughman's lunch or a thick-cut ham sandwich). If you have a chutney-loving friend, you could give him or her one jar of this recipe and one jar of the Tomato chutney on pages 20–21.

Makes: three 450g *(1lb)* jars

Preparation time: 15 minutes, plus 24 hours steeping

Cooking time: about 45 minutes

Ingredients

1kg *(2lb 4oz)* apples – you can use cooking or eating apples but, if you choose the latter, pick a flavourful variety such as Cox or Reinette
115g *(4oz)* salt
600ml *(1 pint)* malt vinegar
450g *(1lb)* sultanas
225g *(8oz)* raisins
6 garlic cloves
25g *(1oz)* fresh red chilli, chopped
1kg *(2lb 4oz)* brown sugar
60g *(2¼oz)* mustard seeds
1 tsp ground ginger

Method

1 Peel, core and finely slice the apples, then put them into a large bowl. Stir in the salt and leave, covered with a clean tea towel, for 24 hours.

2 Drain the apples and put them into a large stainless-steel saucepan, add half the vinegar and simmer gently over a low heat until tender. Remove from the heat and leave to cool.

3 Chop the sultanas, raisins, garlic, chilli as finely as possible – it is easiest to do this in a food processor, although you can do it by hand, especially if you are skilled with a mezzaluna. Alternatively, you can use a sharp knife.

4 In a small saucepan, add the sugar and pour in the remaining vinegar, then place over a gentle heat and simmer for 5 minutes to make a syrup. Using a pestle and mortar, grind the mustard seeds and ginger together and add them to the syrup. Simmer for a further 5 minutes, pour onto the cooled apples and add the chopped raisin mixture. Stir everything together thoroughly.

5 Place the chutney on a low heat and simmer gently until it thickens (this will take between 10 and 20 minutes), pour into hot, sterilized jars then seal and label. The chutney will be ready to eat after a week but will keep for a year if unopened. Once opened, keep unrefrigerated and use within two months.

Piccalilli

Crunchy, mustardy pickled vegetables may seem old-fashioned today, but do try them – this lively recipe leaves the vegetables with plenty of crunch and a delicious sweet-and-sour flavour; it will be popular with those who find many chutneys and pickles bland. The fiery English mustard taste is modified by the Demerara sugar, and the spices impart a subtlety that you won't find in the many commercial brands of this traditional favourite.

Makes: four 450g *(1lb)* jars

Preparation time: 15 minutes, plus overnight steeping

Cooking time: about 30 minutes

Ingredients

1 large cucumber
3 courgettes
handful of green beans
1 small cauliflower
8 pickling onions, peeled
2 tbsp salt
900ml *(1½ pints)* distilled white malt vinegar
1 tbsp mustard seeds
1 tsp black peppercorns
3 fresh green chillies
1 tbsp mustard powder
1 tbsp turmeric
2 tsp ground ginger
115g *(4oz)* Demerara sugar
2 tsp plain flour

Method

1 Rinse all the vegetables in cold water and pat them dry. Cut the unpeeled cucumber into 1cm *(½in)* cubes, thinly slice the courgettes, and cut the beans into thirds. Break up the cauliflower into small florets and place all the vegetables, including the whole onions, into a large bowl. Sprinkle with the salt and pour enough water over to cover. Then cover the bowl with a clean tea towel and leave overnight.

2 Drain the vegetables and rinse them with clean water. Put 600ml *(1 pint)* of the vinegar, with the mustard seeds, peppercorns and chillies, into a large stainless-steel saucepan, place over a low heat and bring slowly to the boil. Cover and simmer for 10 minutes. Strain the mixture, discard the spices, then return the vinegar to the saucepan.

3 In a small bowl, mix together the mustard powder, turmeric, ginger, sugar, flour and the rest of the vinegar. Mix thoroughly until the mixture is completely smooth. Add this mixture to the hot, spiced vinegar and bring to the boil, stirring constantly (the flour will thicken the mixture slightly, but you need to stir it to ensure that no lumps form). Now add the vegetables and simmer gently for 10 minutes, stirring it every now and then.

4 Remove from the heat and allow the piccalilli to cool completely before decanting it into sterilized jars. Seal, label and store in a cool, dark place. The piccalilli will be ready to eat after a week, and will keep unopened for three months. Once opened, keep refrigerated and eat within two weeks.

Tomato chutney

Tomatoes are to chutney what strawberries are to jam, and this glorious red concoction is a spicy classic. It goes with anything, and looks beautiful – good qualities in a food gift! Although you should really leave it to mature for two months before opening the jar, it will taste fine after a month if you really can't wait. The mustard powder in the recipe gives this chutney a powerful tang; if you prefer a milder tomato taste don't use the full quantity but cut it back to 15g (½oz).

Makes: four 450g *(1lb)* jars

Preparation time: 10 minutes

Cooking time: about 30–45 minutes

Ingredients

1.5 kg *(3lb 5oz)* ripe tomatoes
900g *(2lb)* cooking apples
225g *(8oz)* onions, peeled
60g *(2¼oz)* pickling spice
25g *(1oz)* mustard powder
25g *(1oz)* salt
300ml *(10fl oz)* distilled white malt vinegar
225g *(8oz)* sultanas
350g *(12oz)* brown sugar
3 garlic cloves, peeled and chopped

Method

1 Peel the tomatoes by using a sharp knife to score the bottom of each with a cross, then placing in a bowl of boiling water. Leave for a minute, then drain off the water, leave the tomatoes to cool for a minute, then peel off the skins. Chop the flesh roughly. Peel, core and chop the apples into large chunks, and dice the onions into smallish pieces.

2 Put the tomatoes, apples and onions into a large stainless-steel saucepan. Tie the pickling spice into a small piece of cloth or muslin and add to the mixture. Place over a gentle heat and bring to a simmer.

3 After the tomatoes have simmered for 10 minutes, put the mustard and salt in a small bowl, mix with a little vinegar, then stir into the tomato mixture.

4 When the ingredients have softened, add the sultanas, sugar, garlic and remaining vinegar. Keep simmering, stirring constantly, until smooth and thick.

5 Pour into hot, sterilized jars, seal and label. Ideally, this chutney should be left for two months before using. Unopened it will keep for a year. Once opened, keep refrigerated and eat within a month.

Apricot & almond jam

If you have a yen to make jam but it's not the season for any of the classic fruits or berries, this syrupy dried-fruit jam is the answer. It's very quick to make: although you have to soak the apricots to prepare them, this doesn't mean any extra work on your part, only a little extra time before you actually start to cook. The blanched almonds make for a slightly Eastern flavour combination in the finished jam, although you can leave them out if you prefer a smooth texture. The smaller, harder Hunza dried apricots you can sometimes buy in specialist food shops will give this jam a depth of taste that you won't get from the blander, plumper supermarket apricots – but whichever you use, the end result will be delicious.

Makes: four 450g *(1lb)* jars

Preparation time: 10 minutes, plus 24 hours soaking

Cooking time: about 45 minutes

Ingredients

775g *(1lb 11oz)* dried apricots
2 litres *(3½ pints)* water
1 kg *(2lb 4oz)* cooking apples
2 lemons
1.5kg *(3lb 5oz)* granulated sugar
115g *(4oz)* almonds, halved and blanched

Method

1 Place the dried apricots and water into a large bowl, cover with a clean tea towel and leave for 24 hours.

2 When you are ready to cook the jam, peel and core the apples, chop roughly and put the pieces into a large preserving pan. Drain the apricot liquid into the pan and cook the apples until they are soft and fluffy.

3 Zest the lemons and squeeze them. Add the zest and juice to the apples, together with the apricots, and boil for about 10 minutes. Put the granulated sugar in an ovenproof bowl and warm slightly in a very low oven.

4 Stir the sugar into the apple mixture and boil rapidly, stirring often to prevent it sticking. After 15 minutes, drop a teaspoonful of the mixture onto a saucer, leave for a minute, and see if it sets. If it does not, boil for another 5 minutes, then try again. As soon as the setting point is reached, remove the pan from the heat and leave to cool for 5 minutes.

5 When the jam has cooled a little, stir in the almonds and ladle into warm, sterilized jars. Seal immediately, then label. This jam is ready to eat as soon as it is cool. Unopened it will keep for a year. Once opened, keep refrigerated and use within two months.

Quince jelly

Cooking quinces have a scent like nothing else – deep and rich, and very distinctive. Quinces are hard to find in the shops, so they're a precious commodity, but if you have a quince tree or can get a supply from a friend, make as much of this jelly as you can: it's the very best way to keep that wonderful smell and flavour going for a few months. This jelly takes a little – though only a little – more effort than some others, because quinces are hard and take a while to cook thoroughly, but the results are well worth the trouble. Pot the jelly into small jars, as befits its luxurious status.

Makes: seven 200g *(7oz)* jars

Preparation time: 15–20 minutes, plus 4 hours draining

Cooking time: about 2 hours

Ingredients
1.8kg *(4lb)* quinces
3.5 litres *(6¼ pints)* of water
4 tbsp fresh lemon juice
granulated sugar

Method

1 Wash the quinces, cut them up roughly and place the pieces in a large stainless-steel saucepan with 2.5 litres *(4½ pints)* of the water. Add the lemon juice, cover and simmer until the fruit is soft and tender. This will take about an hour.

2 Put the fruit and juice into a muslin jelly bag and suspend it over a large bowl. Leave to drain into the bowl for 3 hours. Do not squeeze the juice out, because this will lead to a cloudy jelly.

3 Put the strained juice to one side, put the drained quince pulp back into the cleaned saucepan, then add the remaining water. Simmer for another 30 minutes, then pour into a jelly bag and leave to strain for an hour. Next, combine the two lots of juices from the first and the second processes.

4 Measure the amount of liquid produced and to each 600ml *(1 pint)* of juice add 450g *(1lb)* of sugar. Place the juice and sugar in a large saucepan and heat very gently until the sugar has dissolved. When the sugar has dissolved and the jelly is clear, boil the jelly for 20 minutes. Take a teaspoonful of the mixture and drop it onto a clean saucer to see if the jelly sets. If it has not reached the setting stage, boil for another 5 minutes then try again. As soon as the setting point has been reached, remove the jelly from the heat.

5 Ladle the jelly into hot, sterilized jars, then seal and label. This jelly will keep for a year unopened. Once opened, keep refrigerated and use within one month.

Chunky marmalade with whisky

Even people who aren't keen jam-makers usually try to make marmalade once or twice. This version is richly flavoured with whisky and a touch of treacle. It's easy to make and tasty to eat (and, incidentally, if you're a keen cake-maker, it also makes an absolutely unforgettable marmalade sponge). The sour Seville oranges are in season only very early in the year, so if you know a lot of marmalade-lovers it is worth doubling these quantities so that you have plenty to give away.

Makes: six 450g *(1lb)* jars

Preparation time: 15 minutes, plus 30 minutes cooling

Cooking time: about 2 hours

Ingredients

1.3kg *(3lb)* Seville oranges
3 sweet oranges
3 lemons
3 litres *(5¼ pints)* water
2.7kg *(6lb)* granulated sugar
1 tbsp black treacle
6 tbsp whisky

Method

1 Thoroughly wash all the oranges and lemons and place them whole in a large preserving pan. Add the water, cover the pan and simmer gently over a low heat until the skin of the fruit pierces easily with the point of a knife and the fruit feels tender. This may take up to an hour. Remove from the heat and leave to cool.

2 Take each fruit out and roughly cut it up (depending on how chunky you'd like your marmalade to be) being careful to scrape out and save the pips. Put the pips back into the cooking liquid and put the chopped fruit into a separate bowl.

3 Place the pan on a high heat and boil the cooking liquid until it has reduced by half.

4 Strain the reduced cooking liquid into a preserving pan, add the chopped fruit and slowly bring back to the boil. Stir in the sugar and black treacle and boil rapidly for about 20 minutes. Drop a teaspoonful of the marmalade onto a saucer to see if it sets. If it is not quite ready, boil the mixture for another minute or two and try again. As soon as the setting point is reached, take the marmalade off the heat.

5 Pour into hot, sterilized jars, then, taking a small spoon, stir a tablespoonful of whisky into each. Seal immediately. The marmalade can be eaten immediately, but will keep for a year or more unopened. Once opened, use within two months.

Cranberry & orange preserve

Delicious with a traditional roast turkey meal, and good with cold meat or cheese of any kind, this preserve is a pretty colour and looks lovely spooned into a glass dish on the Christmas table or other festive occasion. And it's a boon to a hard-pressed cook who has dealt with every other aspect of a dinner that always seems twice the work of any other they'll cook all year. Make plenty of jars so that you can distribute them with a free hand at Christmas time and other special occasions.

Method

1 Put the cranberries in a large, stainless-steel saucepan and cover with the orange juice. (If using frozen cranberries, make sure they are thoroughly defrosted before you start.)

2 Simmer the mixture over a gentle heat until the berries start to pop open, then simmer for a further 5 minutes. In the meantime, warm the granulated sugar slightly in a large heatproof bowl in a very low oven.

3 Stir the warmed sugar into the cranberry mixture and simmer slowly for another 5 minutes until the sugar has dissolved and the mixture has thickened slightly.

4 Remove from the heat, ladle into hot, sterilized jars, then seal and label. The preserve can be eaten immediately, but unopened it will last for six months (although it's unlikely that it will remain uneaten that long). Once opened, keep refrigerated and use within one month.

Makes: four 200g *(7oz)* jars

Preparation time: 5 minutes

Cooking time: about 15–20 minutes

Ingredients

500g *(1lb 2oz)* fresh cranberries
(if you can't find fresh, use frozen, which
are more widely available)
350ml *(12fl oz)* freshly squeezed
orange juice
200g *(7oz)* granulated sugar

Cucumber relish

Fresh-tasting and pretty, this green relish is speckled with red from the peppers in the recipe, and is popular with those who like something a little lighter and less sweet than traditional chutneys.

Makes: four 450g *(1lb)* jars

Preparation time: 15–20 minutes, plus 4 hours steeping

Cooking time: 10 minutes

Ingredients
350g *(12oz)* celery
1 green pepper
1 red pepper
350g *(12oz)* onions
2 large cucumbers
25g *(1oz)* salt
350g *(12oz)* granulated sugar
350ml *(12fl oz)* distilled white malt vinegar
1 tbsp celery seeds
1 tbsp mustard seeds

Method

1 Trim and de-string the celery, de-seed the peppers and peel the onions, then chop all the vegetables roughly and mix them together in a large bowl.

2 Pour the salt over the vegetables, cover them with water and leave to stand for 4 hours. Drain thoroughly in a colander, pressing down slightly to get rid of any excess liquid.

3 In a stainless-steel saucepan, combine the sugar, vinegar, celery seeds and mustard seeds and slowly bring them to the boil, stirring to dissolve the sugar.

4 When the sugar has dissolved, add the drained vegetables. Stir and simmer gently for 3 minutes. Keep a careful eye on the time and don't cook them for longer; the vegetables should remain crunchy.

5 Pour the relish into hot, sterilized jars, then seal and label immediately. This relish can be eaten straight away, but will improve if left to mature for a few weeks. Unopened, it will last for six months. Once opened, keep refrigerated and use within one month.

Preserved lemons, Moroccan-style

These lemons are an important ingredient in a lot of Middle Eastern cookery. Once they have been thoroughly preserved in the salt, pieces are washed and added to pilafs, couscous, roasted meats and other recipes to give flavour and depth to the dish. They are also washed, cut into small pieces and served as straightforward pickles with snacks. Less mouth-puckeringly sour than fresh lemons, they have a subtlety that can prove quite addictive – and as a present, they have the undoubted advantage of looking very pretty in their large preserving jar.

Makes: one 1.5 litre *(2¾ pint)* jar

Preparation time: 20 minutes, plus 1 month steeping

Cooking time: none required

Ingredients
20 organic, unwaxed lemons
500g *(1lb 2oz)* coarse sea salt
3 bay leaves
2 dried red chillies
1 tbsp coriander seeds

Method

1 Sterilize the jar you will be using for your lemons with boiling water.

2 Take a lemon and cut it almost into quarters lengthways, but leaving the four pieces just attached at the stem end. Cover the cut faces of the lemon thickly with salt, then press it back into the shape of a whole fruit and put it into the pickling jar.

3 Repeat with more lemons until the jar is tightly packed with thickly salted lemons. Sprinkle more salt in as you go, so that the lemons are thickly layered with salt, then add the bay leaves, chillies and coriander seeds between the lemons as you fill the jar.

4 When the jar is full, put the lid on and set it aside. Leave it for three days, but give it a thorough shake whenever you pass it. This is to encourage the lemons to 'give up' their juice into the salt.

5 After four days the lemons will have settled, so open the jar, and fill it with more salted lemons, gently packing them in place, then top up the jar with freshly squeezed lemon juice. It is essential that the lemons are completely covered. Replace the lid. The lemons will be fully preserved after a month, but will keep for over a year. Once the jar has been opened, keep it in the refrigerator and eat within two months.

Make your own labels

A drawn label, even if it is a very simple design, stamps your jams and jellies as products of your own kitchen. Think about different ways to make labels that appeal to you – you could use stamping or stencils, or try beautiful lettering if you have pretty handwriting, maybe even give yourself a brand if you're working on a production line of presents for a special occasion. The designs below can be scanned or photocopied onto any style of paper, and you can make jar tops out of soft paper fastened with string to match the identifying labels.

You will need

thick photocopy paper and glue, or sticky-backed label paper coloured pencil rubber bands, coloured

soft paper in a colour of your choice (optional) string or thin ribbon (optional)

Method

1 Photocopy any of the designs shown onto thick paper, or directly onto sticky-backed label paper if you don't want to use glue.

2 Colour parts of the patterns or leave them plain if you prefer. Write an identifier for the jam or jelly on the label before sticking it onto the jar, and don't forget to add a date and, if necessary, a 'best before' date, too.

3 To make a matching top for the jar, photocopy the same pattern onto soft paper and cut out a circle 3cm *(1¼in)* larger than the diameter of the jar top. Fix it on top of the jar with a rubber band or, more decoratively, with coloured string or thin ribbon, wrapped around and tied tightly.

Coordinate your patterns

If you would like your jars and bottles to have a polished look, you can choose a fabric for the jar tops and photocopy or print it out for card labels tied onto the jars as identifiers. In these examples we took some 1970s-style fabrics and used them to top the jars. Labels in the same patterns coordinated the jars and bottles. You could also use some patterns and some plain colours to good effect.

You will need

template of your choice (see below)
patterned or plain card
craft knife or small, sharp pair of scissors
coloured ribbon or string
coloured pen or pencil

Method

1 To make decanter-style card labels, choose a template (see below) and trace the shape onto patterned or plain card, enlarging it a little if it looks too small for the jar or bottle you are giving.

2 Cut it out with a craft knife or a small, sharp pair of scissors.

3 Thread some ribbon or a length of coloured string through one of the holes, write a greeting on one side of the label and an identifier on the other – for example, "Limoncello" and the year of making. Add a best before date, then tie the label around the neck of the jar or bottle.

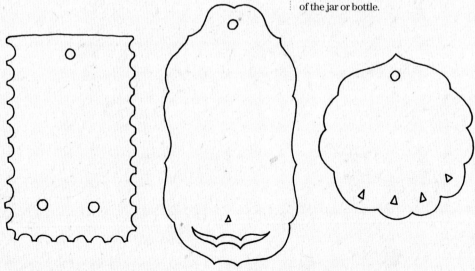

A gift of the recipe

Why not give the recipe along with the jam or jelly? Here is a simple, one-sheet way of folding a piece of paper to form its own envelope. You simply choose a paper patterned on one side and plain on the other, trim it to the size of an A4 sheet if necessary, and write the recipe on the plain side. Fold it up as shown in the steps below and hand it over along with your gift, or slip it into the box or wrapping.

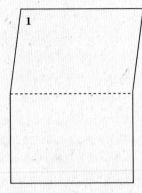

You will need

A4 paper, patterned on one side and plain on the other

Method

1 Write your recipe on a standard letter-sized sheet of paper. If you want to use patterned paper, you may have to trim a sheet to the right size. Then fold it in half horizontally and unfold, leaving a clean central crease.

2 Fold the top left and bottom right corners of the paper in towards the centre fold.

3 Fold the left single edge over into the folded-in edge of the triangle, as shown. Repeat with the single edge on the upper right.

4 Fold in the top and bottom flaps to the centre, as shown. Tuck the corners into the folded 'pockets' created as you do so.

5 You should now have a neat finished envelope with the corners tucked in. You could write the name of the recipient on the right (unfolded) side.

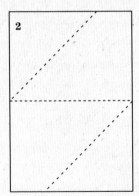

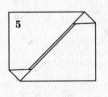

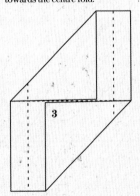

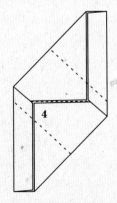

Christina x

Posting jars prettily & safely

If you are sending a present of two or more jars of homemade delicacies, it's nice to create an attractive impression as soon as the box is opened. This way of sending them both protects the jars from breaking en route to their recipient and also looks good. If you can find wood shavings to finish off the packing (you can buy them in craft or some hardware shops), your package will look even better.

You will need

patterned wrapping paper
pencil
scissors
sheets of corrugated card, coloured or plain
glue
coloured string or narrow ribbon

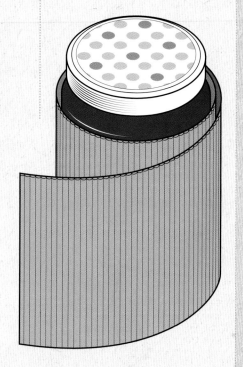

Method

1 Create some patterned tops for your jars by drawing around the jar lids on the wrong side of the wrapping paper with a pencil, then simply cutting out the circles and sticking them onto the lids.

2 Make a sleeve from corrugated card for each jar. Measure the circumference of the jar (you can use a piece of string to measure how long it is around) and cut a strip of corrugated card to the depth of the jar and 2.5cm *(1in)* longer than the circumference.

3 Wrap the card, corrugated side out, around the jar and neatly stick the ends together, overlapping them slightly. You can tie coloured string or narrow ribbon around the centre of each jar for a final touch.

4 Arrange the jars neatly in a solid box and pack any gaps tightly with wood shavings so that the jars cannot move around in transit.

Cakes & Biscuits

Cakes and biscuits are the ultimate eat-now present, whether you are bringing a treat to a children's tea or you have promised to provide dessert for a grown-up dinner party. The selection in this chapter offers enough scope to cover both sorts of occasion, from brownies and cheesecake to biscuits and cupcakes and, with the exception of the fruit cake (which is more than delicious enough to justify the extra effort), they are all quick to mix and bake. Some need to be eaten the day that they are made, others will keep for a little longer – although anything that tastes as good as these recipes probably won't last beyond the day it's baked.

Cherry-topped fruit cake

A fruit cake is one of the great crowd-pleaser gifts: almost everyone likes it and it's a boon to a busy host. This rich recipe has an exotic, almost Creole flavour. It will keep for two or three months in an airtight container, and can be made a week or two in advance of giving without coming to any harm. The glacé cherry topping used here can be changed for a glazed nut version if you prefer.

Makes: one 20cm *(8in)* round cake

Preparation time:
15–20 minutes, plus overnight maceration and 1 hour cooling

Cooking time: 4–4 ½ hours

Ingredients

225g *(8oz)* unsalted butter, plus extra for greasing
280g *(10oz)* sultanas
280g *(10oz)* raisins
280g *(10oz)* currants
115g *(4oz)* glacé cherries
60g *(2¼oz)* blanched almonds, chopped
5 tbsp brandy or rum, according to taste
225g *(8oz)* plain flour
½ tsp ground nutmeg
½ tsp mixed spice
225g *(8oz)* muscovado sugar
4 large eggs
1 tbsp black treacle
2 lemons

For the topping
225g *(8oz)* glacé cherries, halved
2 tbsp apricot conserve

Method

1 Take a 20cm *(8in)* round cake tin, at least 7cm *(2¾in)* deep, and line it with buttered greaseproof paper.

2 Halve the glacé cherries, then put all the dried fruit and the almonds into a large bowl. Stir in the brandy or rum. Cover the bowl with a tea towel and leave overnight.

3 When you are ready to make the cake, preheat the oven to 140°C/275°F/Gas Mark 1. Sift the flour, nutmeg and mixed spice into a mixing bowl and, in another bowl, beat the remaining butter with the sugar until the mixture is light and fluffy.

4 Beat the eggs until they begin to foam, then beat them into the butter and sugar mixture, a little at a time. When all the egg has been added, gently fold in the flour mixture, then add the fruit and the treacle. Zest the lemons and add the zest to the cake mix. Lightly mix everything together.

5 Spoon the mixture into the prepared tin and lay a circle of greaseproof paper over the top of the tin to stop the cake burning. Place on a low shelf in the oven. After 4 hours, put a skewer into the cake's centre – if it comes out very sticky, bake the cake for an additional half hour. The top should be slightly springy to the touch.

6 Remove from the oven and cool in the tin for an hour, then transfer it to a wire rack. When it is cold, arrange the halved cherries on top, warm some apricot conserve and brush it over them, then leave to set before wrapping. If the cake isn't going to be eaten for a few days, wrap in foil until you are ready to give or serve it. It will keep for up to three months in an airtight container.

Stem ginger cake

Lighter than an old-fashioned gingerbread, this cake features chunks of stem ginger to give each slice a little extra bite. This is a plain but elegant confection, which would be good for a coffee morning. If you want it to have a little more visual impact, try the iced option given as a variation at the end of the recipe – rich cream-cheese icing transforms it from delicious but restrained to a fitting dessert for almost any occasion.

Makes: one 450g *(1lb)* loaf

Preparation time: 15 minutes

Cooking time: 30 minutes

Ingredients

115g *(4oz)* unsalted butter, plus extra for greasing
225g *(8oz)* self-raising flour
½ tsp bicarbonate of soda
5 tbsp golden granulated sugar
1–2 tsp ground ginger
pinch of salt
2 tsp golden syrup
2 eggs, separated
2 tbsp milk
115g *(4oz)* stem ginger, chopped, plus extra slices to decorate

Method

1 Preheat the oven to 180°C/350°F/Gas Mark 4. Grease a 450g *(1lb)* loaf tin and line the base with baking paper.

2 Mix together the dry ingredients in a large bowl and make a well in the centre. Melt the remaining butter and the syrup gently, then remove from the heat and add the egg yolks, stirring constantly.

3 Pour the mixture into the dry ingredients and combine. Whisk the egg whites lightly and fold into the mixture. Stir in the milk to make a soft batter, then gently fold in the chopped stem ginger.

4 Pour the mixture into the tin and level the surface. Bake in the middle of the oven for 30 minutes. After 15 minutes, pull out the oven shelf and quickly arrange the stem ginger on the cake. Return it to the oven, turning it to brown evenly.

5 Check the cake is cooked by inserting a skewer into the centre; if it comes out clean, remove the cake from the oven and transfer to a wire rack. Turn out of the tin and leave to cool completely before storing. This cake is best eaten the day after it is made, but will keep for several days in an airtight container.

Variation

If you prefer an iced, filled cake, cut the cake in half horizontally and fill with a layer of ginger marmalade. Make a topping by mixing 115g *(4oz)* icing sugar with 115g *(4oz)* half-fat soft cheese. Spread this icing on top of the cooled cake and decorate with chopped stem ginger.

Lemon & lavender biscuits

Light and crisp, these lemon biscuits are given an unusual twist with the addition of a small quantity of lavender buds. The lavender can be used dried or fresh; the combination of the two quintessentially Mediterranean flavours is delicious and slightly unexpected. A box of these would make an elegant gift. Try the variations – they replace the lavender with chopped thyme or rosemary, for an equally intriguing but slightly more 'herbal' taste – or bake a mixed batch to see which you prefer.

Makes: about 20 cookies

Preparation time: 20 minutes, plus 30 minutes chilling

Cooking time: 10–12 minutes

Ingredients

175g *(6oz)* plain flour, plus extra for dusting
115g *(4oz)* ground almonds
1 tsp baking powder
1 lemon
5 tbsp unsalted butter, softened, plus extra for greasing
175g *(6oz)* caster sugar
1 tbsp soured cream
1 tbsp lavender buds

Method

1 Preheat the oven to 180°C/350°F/Gas Mark 4 and position two oven racks in the middle of the oven. Grease and flour two baking sheets.

2 Mix together the flour, ground almonds and baking powder. Zest the lemon and squeeze it.

3 In a separate bowl, cream together the butter, sugar and lemon zest. Beat in the lemon juice, soured cream and lavender, then mix in the dry ingredients to form a stiff dough. Cover with clingfilm and refrigerate for 30 minutes.

4 Uncover the dough and knead it a little until it becomes malleable. Roll it out on a lightly floured surface to a thickness of 5mm *(¼in)*. Use a 7cm *(2¾in)* round cutter to stamp out the biscuits. Gather the dough scraps, re-roll out and cut biscuits until all the dough is used.

5 Place the biscuits on the prepared baking sheets, placing them 2.5cm *(1in)* apart to allow for expansion during cooking. Bake in the preheated oven for 10–12 minutes, or until lightly golden, rotating the sheets halfway through the cooking time for even baking.

6 Remove from the oven and leave the biscuits to cool slightly before transferring to wire racks. These biscuits are best eaten the day they are made, but will keep for several days in an airtight container.

Variation

Replace the lavender with 1 tsp chopped rosemary or thyme leaves.

Millionaire's shortbread

This is a classic traybake: rich shortbread topped off with layers of caramel and chocolate. Children invariably love it, while their parents can be comforted by the fact that under all that chocolate and toffee is a satisfying shortbread base. This recipe is better than the often delicious versions you can buy in the shops: the difference lies in the delectable crunch of the shortcake base, which commercially made shortbread, however good, never quite matches.

Makes: 16 squares

Preparation time: 15 minutes, plus 1 hour cooling/setting

Cooking time: 20–30 minutes

Ingredients

For the base
115g *(4oz)* unsalted butter, diced, plus extra for greasing
175g *(6oz)* plain flour
25g *(1oz)* golden caster sugar
½ tsp vanilla extract
1 egg yolk

For the toffee
175g *(6oz)* unsalted butter
175g *(6oz)* caster sugar
4 tbsp golden syrup
400ml *(14fl oz)* canned condensed milk

For the topping
200g *(7oz)* dark chocolate

Method

1 Preheat the oven to 180°C/350°F/Gas Mark 4. Lightly grease a baking tin measuring 20 x 20cm *(8 x 8in)*.

2 Put the flour and sugar in a mixing bowl and rub in the remaining butter until the mixture resembles breadcrumbs. Mix the vanilla extract with the egg yolk in a separate bowl and stir into the dry ingredients to bind to a firm dough.

3 Shape the dough into a rough square and flatten it slightly, then press into the base of the prepared baking tin and prick the surface with a fork. Bake for about 10–15 minutes until golden and firm. Set aside to cool.

4 To make the toffee layer, place the ingredients in a saucepan and stir over a low heat until the butter has melted. Bring the mixture to a high simmer, so that it is bubbling but not spitting, and cook for 5–8 minutes, stirring constantly, until it is caramel-coloured, thick and fudge-like. It is ready when a knife drawn across the back of the toffee-covered spoon leaves a clear line in the toffee. Pour it over the cold shortbread in an even layer and leave to cool.

5 While the toffee is setting, break the chocolate into pieces and melt it in a heatproof bowl set over a saucepan of simmering water. Pour the melted chocolate over the toffee and leave to set. When cool, cut into 5cm *(2in)* squares and store in an airtight container until ready to serve. It is best eaten the day it is made, but will keep for several days if necessary.

Foolproof brownies

The perfect brownie can prove to be elusive for the home-baker: too many recipes come out of the oven a little too dry or a little too squidgy, or even a little too original, when what you were after was the classic rich and fudgy treat. This version is lusciously foolproof, turning out the perfect mixture of a slightly crisp top and an interior that is still a little gooey, and with the chopped dates adding an extra but by no means unwelcome touch.

Makes: 12–14 bars

Preparation time: 15 minutes, plus 1 hour cooling

Cooking time: 20 minutes

Ingredients

175g *(6oz)* unsalted butter, plus extra for greasing
300g *(10½oz)* dark chocolate (this should be 70% cocoa solids to get the requisite luscious quality in your brownies)
175g *(6oz)* soft brown sugar
4 large eggs
3 tbsp single cream
115g *(4oz)* ground almonds
¼ tsp salt
115g *(4oz)* self-raising flour
115g *(4oz)* dates, chopped
icing sugar, for dusting (optional)

Method

1 Preheat the oven to 190°C/375°F/Gas Mark 5 and grease a brownie tin (preferably non-stick) that measures 34 x 20cm *(13½ x 8in)*, and 3cm *(1¼in)* deep.

2 Gently melt the chocolate with the remaining butter in a large heatproof bowl set over a saucepan of simmering water. Remove from the heat, add the sugar and stir to combine.

3 Add the eggs to the chocolate mixture, one by one, beating after each addition to give a glossy mixture. Mix in the cream. Fold in the ground almonds and salt, then sift over the flour and fold in gently without overmixing. Gently fold in the chopped dates.

4 Pour the mixture into the prepared tin and bake in the preheated oven for 20 minutes, or until the edges have shrunk from the sides and the top is just beginning to crack. Run a knife around the edge of the tin, then leave the cake to cool in the tin completely before cutting it into bars. If you are giving a batch as a gift, dust with icing sugar before wrapping. Brownies are most delicious eaten as soon as they have cooled, but will keep for two days in an airtight container. If kept longer than this they tend to dry out a little.

Spiced choc-chip cookies

A touch of spice adds a extra depth of flavour to these classic chocolate-chip cookies. If you're not a fan of nutmeg, you could add ground cinnamon or mixed spice to the cookie dough instead. Use good-quality chocolate chips made from real chocolate. If you can't find any that are suitable, chop a bar of chocolate into small pieces instead.

Makes: between 15 and 20 cookies, depending on size

Preparation time: 20 minutes, plus 1¼ hours cooling/chilling

Cooking time: 10–12 minutes

Ingredients
225g *(8oz)* unsalted butter, softened
200g *(7oz)* light muscovado sugar
175g *(6oz)* golden caster sugar
2 eggs, beaten
350g *(12oz)* plain flour
1 level tsp baking powder
1 level tsp bicarbonate of soda
pinch of salt
150g *(5½oz)* dark chocolate chips
½ tsp freshly grated nutmeg
1 tsp cocoa powder

Method

1 Preheat the oven to 180°C/350°F/Gas Mark 4. Have two non-stick baking sheets ready.

2 Cream the butter and both sugars until light and fluffy. Add the beaten eggs a little at a time. In a separate bowl, mix together the dry ingredients and fold them into the egg mixture. Add the chocolate chips and stir to combine. The mixture should make a firm dough.

3 Wrap the dough in clingfilm and then refrigerate for about 15 minutes.

4 Divide the dough into 50g *(1¾oz)* portions for large, American-style cookies (or use less to make smaller ones). Mix the nutmeg and cocoa powder thoroughly on a plate, roll the dough pieces into balls, flatten slightly, then roll each piece briefly through the cocoa mixture.

5 Place the cookies about 5cm *(2in)* apart on the baking sheets and cook for 10–12 minutes, turning the sheets halfway through the cooking time for even baking.

6 Remove the cookies from the oven, cool them on the sheets, then transfer them to wire racks until completely cold. Store in an airtight container. These cookies are most delicious eaten straight after baking, but will keep for several days in an airtight container.

Variation

For cookies with a slight citrus tang, add the grated zest of 1 orange at the same time as the eggs.

Madeira cake

Madeira cake has, unfairly, a slightly dull reputation – old-fashioned, but without the glamour of nostalgia. However, a freshly baked Madeira cake has few rivals for taste. Subtly lemony and elegantly topped with crystallized lemon rind, this version should make a welcome addition to any tea table and its merits will ensure that it doesn't linger there for very long. It makes a good gift for people who are slightly suspicious of heavily iced and decorated cakes: with a Madeira cake, what you see is what you get, and what you get is pure flavour and a buttery texture.

Makes: one 18cm *(7in)* cake

Preparation time: 15 minutes, plus 30 minutes–1 hour cooling

Cooking time: 1½ hours

Ingredients
175g *(6oz)* unsalted butter, plus extra for greasing
225g *(8oz)* self-raising flour
¼ tsp salt
175g *(6oz)* caster sugar
1 lemon
4 eggs, beaten
crystallized lemon rind, to decorate

Method

1 Preheat the oven to 160°C/325°F/Gas Mark 3. Grease and line a round cake tin, 18cm *(7in)* in diameter, with baking paper.

2 Sift the flour and salt together. In a separate bowl, cream the remaining butter with the sugar until light and fluffy. In another bowl, zest the lemon and add it to the beaten eggs, then add the egg mixture to the butter and sugar a little at a time, adding a tablespoonful of the flour mixture between each addition of egg.

3 When all the egg is incorporated, fold in any remaining flour and mix gently.

4 Spoon the mixture into the prepared tin and bake in the middle of the preheated oven for 1 hour. After 30 minutes, gently and quickly place the crystallized lemon rind on top of the cake without removing it from the oven.

5 After the first hour, turn the cake around so that it cooks evenly, and reduce the temperature to 150°C/300°F/Gas Mark 2. Bake for a further 30 minutes, or until the top is risen and golden brown. Check the centre is cooked by inserting a skewer. If it comes out clean, your cake is done.

6 Remove from the oven and leave the cake to cool in the tin for 5 minutes before turning out onto a wire rack to finish cooling. This cake is delicious eaten while still warm, but will keep for up to a week in an airtight container.

Cinnamon biscuits

These are the sort of flat, tidy biscuits that are easy to cut into elaborate shapes and they also take iced decoration very well. If you want to make edible Christmas decorations or a personalized cookie 'birthday card', this is the mixture you should choose. Flavoured with cinnamon rather than the more traditional ginger, they're also crisp and delicious to eat. And, finally, they are also a good choice if you are cooking with small children, because they can make and decorate completely original creations of their own without the level of mess that usually results from one of the less dry, greasier biscuit recipes.

Makes: 12–16 biscuits, depending on the size of your cutters

Preparation time:
15–20 minutes, plus 1 hour chilling

Cooking time: 9–12 minutes

Ingredients
5 tbsp plain flour, plus extra for dusting
25g *(1oz)* golden caster sugar
4 tbsp unsalted butter, diced
pinch of sea salt
½ tsp ground cinnamon
1 medium egg yolk
vegetable oil, for oiling

Method

1 Put the flour, sugar, butter, salt and cinnamon in the bowl of a food processor and process to the consistency of crumbs (alternatively, rub the butter into the dry ingredients with your fingertips).

2 Mix in the egg yolk and shape the dough into a ball. Wrap in clingfilm and refrigerate for 1 hour.

3 Preheat the oven to 190°C/375°F/Gas Mark 5 and lightly oil a baking sheet. Knead the dough until pliable, then thinly roll out on a lightly floured work surface until about 2mm *(1/16in)* thick.

4 Cut out biscuits using a 5cm *(2in)* round biscuit cutter, or any shaped cutters you like, re-rolling the dough pieces as you go until all the mixture has been used.

5 Transfer the biscuits to the prepared baking sheet, spacing them 1cm *(½in)* apart. Bake for 9–12 minutes until lightly golden, then remove from the oven and leave the biscuits to cool on the baking sheet. Transfer them to a plate using a palette knife. They will keep well in a covered container for several days.

Variation

To make festive biscuits, choose star- or leaf-shaped cutters and use a skewer to make a hole near the top of each shape. Drizzle melted chocolate in thin patterns or use writing icing over the cooled biscuits. Carefully thread ribbon through each hole and hang from a Christmas tree or use as decorations on any festive table.

Scottish shortbread round

This very traditional recipe incorporates ground rice, which will give the cooked shortbread an additional crispness. If you're a shortbread enthusiast, it is well worth making your own: fresh from the oven it has a texture and taste that you will not find in any bought version. Absolutely fresh shortbread makes a good gift because it is appropriate at any time – with morning coffee, on the afternoon tea table or accompanying fruit or ice cream at the end of a meal. Always offer it the day it is made; although still tasty, it is never quite as wonderful a day or two later.

Makes: one 22cm *(8½in)* round of shortbread

Preparation time: 10–15 minutes, plus 1 hour cooling/chilling

Cooking time: 45 minutes–1 hour

Ingredients

275g *(9½oz)* cold unsalted butter, cut into cubes, plus extra for greasing
350g *(12oz)* plain flour
115g *(4oz)* caster sugar, plus extra for dusting
75g *(2¾oz)* ground rice
pinch of baking powder

Method

1 Preheat the oven to 180°C/350°F/Gas Mark 4. Grease the base of a 22cm *(8½in)* springform cake tin.

2 Sieve together all the dry ingredients in a large bowl. Rub in the remaining butter with your fingertips until the mixture resembles breadcrumbs. Continue to work it lightly until it forms a dough.

3 Place the dough on the base of the prepared tin and gently shape it into a round 1.5cm *(⅝in)* thick. Roll a rolling pin over the top to give it a smooth surface, then crimp the edge all the way round using the tines of a fork. You can also mark lines for triangular slices of shortbread with a sharp knife. Refrigerate for 5 minutes.

4 Transfer the shortbread on its base to a baking sheet and drop the springform cake ring around it but do not tighten the clip: the ring is just to prevent the shortbread from getting too brown. Bake for 45 minutes–1 hour until lightly golden but cooked through. Sprinkle with a little caster sugar while still hot and leave to cool in the tin. Remove from the tin when completely cold. Shortbread will keep well for up to a week in an airtight tin, although it's most delicious eaten while still warm.

Almond teacakes

Dress these up in a pretty box and they make a great coffee- or tea-time gift. They take barely 30 minutes to beat and bake, and are delicate and delicious with one easily met proviso: they must be eaten the day they are made. The unusual mix of crunchy macadamias and moist almond sponge is delicious – and even if you think you don't like white chocolate, don't be tempted to leave it out; it adds a slight unctuousness that works really well. If you are serving these at home they are especially good with a scoop of vanilla ice cream on the side.

Makes: 24 squares

Preparation time: 10 minutes, plus 1 hour cooling

Cooking time: 20 minutes

Ingredients
115g *(4oz)* unsalted butter, plus extra for greasing
50g *(1¾oz)* good-quality white chocolate, chopped
115g *(4oz)* macadamia nuts, chopped into large pieces
2 large eggs
250g *(9oz)* caster sugar
50g *(1¾oz)* ground almonds
50g *(1¾oz)* plain flour

Method

1 Preheat the oven to 180°C/350°F/Gas Mark 4. Grease a baking tray measuring 30 x 20cm *(12 x 8in)* and line the base with baking paper.

2 Melt the remaining butter in a small saucepan over a low heat, then stir in the chopped chocolate and the macadamia nuts. Stir together until combined.

3 Beat the eggs until pale and frothy, then beat in the sugar to make a light, airy mixture. Using a spatula, gently fold the egg and butter mixtures together until well combined.

4 Sieve the ground almonds and the flour together in a separate bowl, then fold into the egg mixture, keeping movements gentle so that as little air is lost from the mixture as possible. Pour into the prepared baking tray and bake in the middle of the preheated oven for 20 minutes until lightly browned with a crisp crust on the top, but gooey in the centre if you put a skewer or the tip of a knife into it.

5 Remove from the oven and leave in the tin to cool. When the cake is cold, cut into 5cm *(2in)* squares. If you are giving the teacakes as a gift, pack the squares into a box or tin, interleaved with greaseproof paper. These cakes should be eaten on the day they are baked.

Cupcakes

Cupcakes are good for small celebrations – customizable for any occasion, they can be frosted and piped with letters or pictures. A group together can spell out a name or birthday wishes, or they can be studded with individual candles, so they make great little homemade gifts to mark a special occasion. They are best eaten the day they are made.

Makes: 12 cupcakes

Preparation time: 20 minutes

Cooking time: 15 minutes

Ingredients

For the cupcakes
2 eggs
115g *(4oz)* unsalted butter, softened
115g *(4oz)* caster sugar
115g *(4oz)* self-raising flour
1 tsp lemon juice
a few tbsp semi-skimmed milk

For butter icing
5 tbsp butter
175g *(6oz)* icing sugar, sifted
1 tbsp milk, lemon juice or orange juice

To decorate
cake decorations of your choice, such as chocolate buttons, writing icing , candles, hundreds and thousands, or crystallized chopped fruits

Method

1 Preheat the oven to 200°C/400°F/Gas Mark 6. Prepare a 12-hole bun tray with paper cases.

2 Separate the eggs, putting the yolks and whites into separate bowls.

3 Cream the butter and caster sugar together until light and fluffy. Add in a little beaten egg yolk, then a little flour, alternating until all the yolk and flour is used up. Add the lemon juice and stir to incorporate. Whisk the egg whites to soft peaks and, using a metal spoon, lightly fold into the mixture. You want to achieve a soft dropping consistency: if the mixture seems too heavy, add a little milk, a tablespoon at a time, until the mixture easily drops off your mixing spoon.

4 Divide the mixture between the 12 paper cases. Do not overfill the cases: they should be no more than two-thirds full. Even out the surface, and make a slight indentation in the centre.

5 Bake in the middle of the preheated oven for 15 minutes, turning the tin 180 degrees once if necessary. Insert a skewer into a cake; if it comes out clean, the cakes are cooked. If not, reduce the temperature to 180°C/350°F/Gas Mark 4 and allow up to 5 minutes longer. Remove from the oven and transfer the cupcakes to a wire rack while you prepare the icing.

6 Put the butter into a bowl, beat in the icing sugar and then mix in the milk, lemon juice or orange juice. Use the butter icing immediately, while the cakes are still warm. Arrange your chosen decorations on the cakes before the icing sets.

Variations

To make a chocolate ganache topping, break 200g *(7oz)* good-quality dark chocolate (at least 70% cocoa solids) into pieces, then put into a heatproof bowl. Add 200ml *(7fl oz)* double cream, place over a saucepan of simmering water and gently melt together. Remove from the heat and beat hard until the icing becomes glossy and uniform in colour. Spoon over your cupcakes and decorate as before.

To make a glacé icing, use 225g *(8oz)* sifted icing sugar beaten with 2–3 tbsp water and a few drops of food colouring of your choice. Spread or pipe the icing onto the cupcakes and decorate.

If you wish to use writing icing to create patterns, names or messages, wait until the base icing has set.

Cupcakes should be eaten on the day they are baked.

Vanilla & sweet chestnut cheesecake

This uncooked cheesecake is rich and delicious. It makes a lavish teatime treat or a good finale to a dinner. It can be tricky to transport: it is easiest moved on its own large plate, or looks wonderfully impressive on an old-fashioned glass cake stand. (Look for these in charity shops – they will add the ultimate finishing touch to a cake gift.) Keep the cheesecake cool and eat it the day it is made.

Makes: one 20cm *(8in)* cheesecake, serving 8–10 people

Preparation time: 15 minutes, plus 2 hours chilling

Cooking time: 5 minutes

Ingredients

300g *(10½oz)* digestive or amaretti biscuits
150g *(5½oz)* unsalted butter
600g *(1lb 5oz)* cream cheese
450g *(1lb)* mascarpone
1 tsp vanilla extract
juice of 1 lemon
25g *(1oz)* caster sugar (optional)
500g *(1lb 2oz)* tin sweetened chestnut purée slices of marron glacé (optional), to decorate

Method

1 Reduce the biscuits to crumbs in a food processor or place them in a strong plastic bag and crush them with a rolling pin. Melt the butter in a small saucepan. Put the biscuit crumbs in a bowl, add the butter and stir thoroughly. Tip into the base of a 20cm *(8in)* springform cake tin, pressing the biscuit mixture down firmly. Put the tin in the refrigerator while you are making the cheesecake filling.

2 In a separate bowl, beat the cream cheese and mascarpone together until smooth, then add the vanilla extract and lemon juice, and the sugar if you prefer a sweetened cheese mixture. (The chestnut purée is very sweet, so if you don't have a sweet tooth, leave the sugar out.)

3 Spread half the chestnut purée onto the chilled biscuit base. Pour half the cream cheese mixture over the top and level the surface. Use a teaspoon to dot the remaining chestnut purée over the top (you will not be able to spread it) and use a skewer to swirl it into the cheese mixture a little. Top with the remaining cheese mixture and smooth. Cover the tin with clingfilm and refrigerate for at least 2 hours.

4 Shortly before serving (or preparing as a gift), remove the cheesecake from the tin but leave the base underneath to support it, and decorate with the marron glacé slices if using. The cheesecake should be allowed to come to room temperature for 20 minutes before serving. Keep the portions small – the cake is very rich.

Making a box for a cake

This sturdy, lidded box can be reused by the recipient provided that you line it well with greaseproof paper before you put the cake in. The sizing here makes a box 25cm *(10in)* square by 9cm *(3½in)* deep, but can be tailored to fit any contents once you have the hang of basic box-making.

You will need

tracing paper for the template
2 sheets decorative paper, at least the same size as the card (if smaller, glue sheets together to get the right size; leave to dry before cutting)
2 sheets of card, 300gsm weight, measuring at least 63.5 x 76cm *(25 x 30in)*

glue
metal ruler/straight edge
pencil
bone folder or blunt scissor blade
craft knife
cutting board
bulldog clips

Method

1 Size up or photocopy the template to the dimensions given. Now copy it onto tracing paper.

2 Lay the template over the decorative paper, then over the card, to ensure it will fit.

3 Spread a thin layer of glue all over one side of each of the two pieces of card and lay the paper sheets over them, smoothing out any wrinkles or folds before the glue dries.

4 When they are dry, turn the sheets over and draw around the two box templates, the top on one and the base on the other.

5 Rule the folding lines onto the card with a pencil. You can score the folds with a bone folder if you have one, or a blunt scissor

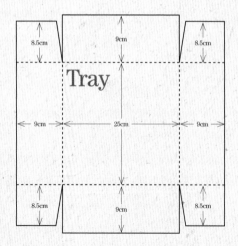

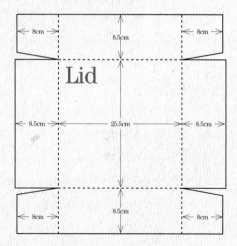

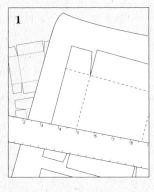

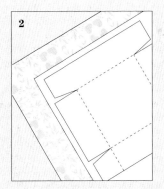

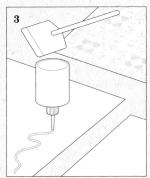

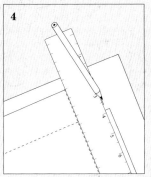

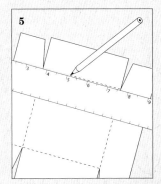

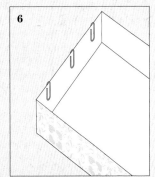

blade if not. Cut around the box shapes with a craft knife, using a straight edge to keep the edges sharp and even.

6 To make up the box, fold up the sides of the base, scoring along the flaps. Fold them into place on the inner edges of the box and glue in place, using paperclips to hold them together until the glue is dry.

7 Repeat to make up the lid of the box. Again, clip the glued flaps in place and leave to dry.

Making a motif-topped carton

These boxes have shaped tops that slot together to close, and can then be simply pulled apart. All three designs share the same basic template; choose whichever of the three patterns you like best to top your carton – there's a heart, a star or a leaf, and the finished cartons are about 15cm *(6in)* square, easily large enough to accommodate half-a-dozen large biscuits or several small cakes.

You will need

A3 photocopying paper
sharp scissors, or craft
knife and cutting board
pencil

1 sheet coloured card,
200gsm weight, measuring
60 x 45cm *(24 x 18in)*
scissors
glue
greaseproof paper or tissue

Method

1 Size up or photocopy the template to the dimensions given onto a large sheet of paper.

2 Cut out the template and draw around it with a pencil onto the wrong side of a sheet of coloured card. Mark the dotted lines with a pencil.

3 Cut out the box with a craft knife and score lightly along the dotted (folding) lines, using one blade of a pair of scissors.

4 Fold up the sides of the box from the base and fold in the tabs. Spread an even layer of glue on each tab and glue it to the inside of the wall of the box adjacent to it.

5 Cut the two slots in the patterned top of the box. Line the box with greaseproof paper or tissue, fill it with your chosen biscuits or cakes, and slot the two sides of the decorative top together to close the box.

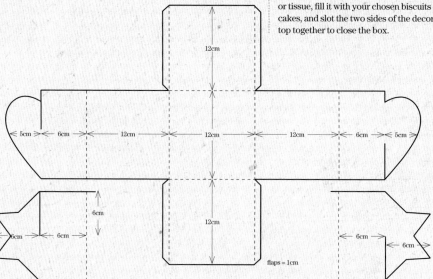

12cm

5cm 6cm 12cm 12cm 12cm 6cm 5cm

6cm

6cm 6cm

12cm

6cm 6cm

flaps = 1cm

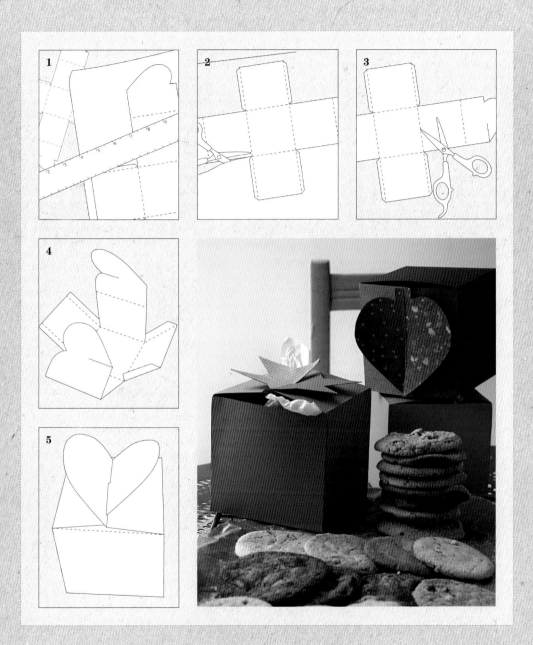

Give the platter

You don't always have to come up with a box, tin or carton for a homemade cake. Look around local charity shops for plates; you can frequently find old-fashioned glass cake stands and platters that can be pressed into service as part of the gift without much extra outlay.

You can also make a composite present with an extra element. Think about:

• Serving up your cake on a sheet of slate (easily washed) with a packet of chalk on the side. Cake eaten, the slate can be used as an in-kitchen reminder list. You can wrap both cake and slate in a loose parcel of cellophane.

• Buy a new cake tin (much more attractive in a shiny silver state), line it with tissue paper, and add your cake.

• Use the same trick with smaller cakes and a shiny new muffin tin.

• Buy a bright but inexpensive coloured chopping board, place the cake on it and wrap in cellophane, as above.

• Scrub an old wooden fruit or seed tray clean and line it with crisp greaseproof paper.

• Use a large, clean flowerpot to present a batch of vanilla cupcakes (you could finish them off and maintain the garden theme by topping each cupcake with a fresh daisy).

• Buy a small trug or woven twig basket and line it with shredded tissue, then put a cake in carefully – it's easiest to do this by putting the cake on a square of greaseproof paper and lifting it into the basket by the corners.

• For a celebration cake, buy a small round 'hatbox'-type container – they're quite widely available from large stationers – and use it instead of a regular cake box. You could write your greetings on wide paper ribbon (also from stationers) and use it to tie a bow round the box, too.

• Small cakes look pretty offered in a set of Chinese bamboo steamer baskets – they usually come in threes. Make cupcakes with three different toppings and put one kind in each steamer basket on a bed of green tissue paper, then tie the baskets together in a stack with ribbon.

• For a teatime gift, buy a pretty tray and put on it a plain but delicious cake (such as the stem ginger or Madeira cakes in this chapter), and put a pack or carton of luxury green tea or smoky lapsang souchong teabags on the side. Then wrap the tray in cellophane as shown opposite.

• Leave a traybake, such as brownies, in its baking tin and wrap the whole thing in a flat paper parcel, using brown paper and coloured string.

Tissue & string

The most basic wrapping of all, but a good resort if you don't have much time – the end effect is out of all proportion to the effort you've put in, and is particularly good with plainish cakes, such as the Madeira or preserved ginger cake recipes. It is worth keeping stores of ribbon and tissue paper at all times – you'll find that having them to hand is nearly as good as having a well-stocked present drawer.

You will need

greaseproof paper
several sheets of tissue
paper in complementary or
contrasting colours
roll of thin ribbon

Method

1 Cut off a piece of greaseproof paper large enough to fold around your cake completely. Place the cake in the centre and wrap it completely, making a double fold on top and tucking the ends in neatly.

2 Layer two or more sheets of tissue paper together. Different colours are attractive – any colour with a white layer outside it will look striking.

3 Lay the cake in the centre of the tissue paper and bring up the sides to make a parcel. Tie with thin ribbon just above the top of the cake, leaving a 'fountain' of tissue paper at the top.

As well as looking pretty, this is a surprisingly protective way of transporting a cake. It is better not to try it with anything that is elaborately iced, however!

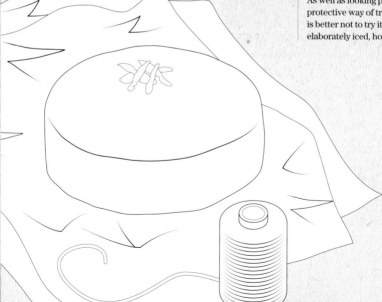

Sweets & Chocolates

Sweets and chocolate treats have many advantages as presents. First, they can usually be cooked in quantity – perfect if you need a lot of small presents that still have a personal note: for a Christmas party, say, or a birthday with a lot of guests when you want to send everyone home with a little something. Second, they are usually easy and quick enough for children to participate in the making – and this can be invaluable, whether you are trying to organize your children to have their own gifts ready or you simply want an enjoyable activity to fill a rainy afternoon. There is a wide selection of recipes to try, from the simplest (and most delicious) chocolate truffles to more old-fashioned confectionery such as coconut ice or buttered Brazil nuts.

Brown sugar fudge

This American -style fudge is also known as Penuche, a name derived from panocha, a sort of raw sugar from Mexico. It is darker in colour than the English variety, and it has a rich caramel fudge flavour. When set, it can be cut into neat squares. Traditionally nuts, such as pecan nuts and walnuts, are added but they can be omitted if you prefer a smoother texture, or simply like your fudge without extra adornment.

Makes: about 50 pieces

Preparation time: 10 minutes, plus 1 hour cooling/setting

Cooking time: 15 minutes

Ingredients

115g *(4oz)* unsalted butter, cut into cubes, plus extra for greasing
55g *(2oz)* pecan or walnut halves
300ml *(10fl oz)* full-fat milk
800g *(1lb 12oz)* light soft brown sugar
2 tsp vanilla extract

Method

1 Grease an 18cm *(7in)* square baking tin. Finely chop the pecan nuts or walnuts. Pour the milk into a large heavy-based saucepan and bring to the boil. Add the sugar and remaining butter and heat gently, stirring all the time, until the sugar has dissolved and the butter melted.

2 Bring the mixture to the boil, cover the pan with a lid and boil gently for 2 minutes. Uncover and continue to boil, stirring occasionally, until a little of the mixture, dropped into a cup of cold water, forms into a ball when rolled between your fingers. If using a sugar thermometer, the mixture should reach 116°C (240°F).

3 Remove the pan from the heat and stir in the vanilla extract and the pecan or walnut pieces. Leave to cool for 5 minutes.

4 Using a wooden spoon, beat the fudge hard until it begins to loss its gloss and becomes thick and creamy. As soon as the mixture starts to look less smooth and slightly grainy, turn it into the prepared tin and leave to cool until half set.

5 When the mixture is half set, mark with a sharp knife into 2.5cm *(1in)* squares and leave to set completely. When the fudge is completely cold and firm, use a sharp knife to cut into the marked squares. Place the squares in paper or foil sweet cases, or pack between layers of baking paper in an airtight container. This fudge will keep in an airtight container for up to a week.

Almond chocolate cups

Little cups of chocolate look very professional but they are surprisingly simple – although quite time-consuming – to make. You will need a small, clean paintbrush and the secret is to coat the paper cases with care. They look very pretty too and, filled with an almond paste, they are a favourite with most chocolate lovers. Children particularly enjoy carefully painting the chocolate into the cases and will happily spend some time at it, so this is a good diversionary treat, too.

Makes: 20 cups

Preparation time: 20–25 minutes, plus 1¼ hours cooling/chilling

Cooking time: 10 minutes

Ingredients

300g *(10½oz)* good-quality dark chocolate
4 tbsp single cream
70g *(2½oz)* ground almonds
¼ tsp almond extract
20 flaked almonds

Method

1 Place 20 foil sweet cases on a small baking tray. Break 100g (3½oz) of the chocolate into pieces in a heatproof bowl, set over a saucepan of simmering water and heat gently until melted. Remove the bowl from the heat and spoon a little of the melted chocolate into the cases, one at a time, spreading it up the sides with a small, clean paintbrush. Return the finished chocolate cases to the tray and chill in the refrigerator for about 1 hour until set.

2 When the chocolate cups have set, carefully peel away the paper cases, pausing to rinse your hands with cold water every so often. Place the cups in clean cases. If you crack a cup as you are removing the case, you can patch it up by using a little of the remaining melted chocolate.

3 Break the remaining chocolate into pieces in the previously used bowl. Add the cream and heat together gently until melted and combined. Remove the bowl from the heat, add the ground almonds and almond extract, and mix well. Leave to cool.

4 Using a piping bag fitted with a large star nozzle, pipe the cooled almond mixture into the chocolate cups (if you don't have a piping bag, improvise one by filling a clean, small plastic bag with the mixture and cutting a tiny hole in one corner to 'pipe' through). Top each chocolate cup with a flaked almond to decorate. Return to the refrigerator and leave to set before placing in an airtight container. The chocolate cups should be stored in the refrigerator and eaten within a week.

Peppermint creams

Children love to make this old-fashioned recipe and the only thing that you need to keep a sharp eye out for is the moment at which the peppermint flavouring is added. Too much and the flavour will be overpowering, rendering the sweets unappetizing. Oil of peppermint is stronger in flavour than extract so, if you are using this, do add it sparingly. Half-dipping the finished peppermints in dark chocolate gives the end product a slightly more sophisticated look.

Makes: about 40 sweets

Preparation time: 20–25 minutes, plus 14–15 hours standing/setting

Cooking time: 5 minutes

Ingredients

1 egg white

450g *(1lb)* fondant icing sugar, plus extra for dusting

1–2 drops oil of peppermint or ½ tsp peppermint extract

2–3 drops green food colouring (optional – you may prefer to leave the sweets pristine white)

150g *(5½oz)* good-quality dark chocolate – it should have at least 50% cocoa solids

Method

1 In a large bowl, whisk the egg white until stiff. Gradually sift in the icing sugar and mix together to form a firm, pliable mixture. Dip the end of a skewer into the oil of peppermint and add 1–2 drops to the mixture to taste or, alternatively, add about ½ tsp peppermint extract to taste. If using, add the food colouring to tint the fondant a pale green and mix it in thoroughly so that the colour is evenly distributed.

2 Turn the fondant onto a clean work surface lightly dusted with icing sugar and knead for 2–3 minutes. Put in a polythene bag and leave at room temperature for about 1 hour.

3 Line a large baking tray with baking paper. Roll out the fondant to 5mm *(¼in)* thickness and, using a 4cm *(1½in)* plain round cutter, cut into rounds. Transfer the rounds to the prepared baking tray and leave in a cool place for about 12 hours, or overnight, until set and dry.

4 Break the chocolate into pieces in a heatproof bowl and place it over a saucepan of simmering water until melted. Remove the bowl from the heat and dip the peppermint rounds into the chocolate to cover one half of each sweet. Lift out quickly, allowing any excess chocolate to drain against the side of the bowl. Place on the prepared baking tray and leave for 1–2 hours until cold and set.

5 Pack between layers of baking paper in an airtight container. The peppermint creams will keep in an airtight container for up to a week.

Cinder toffee

This crunchy toffee gets its name from its appearance, which recalls cinders still glowing in the ashes of a fire. These days it is more commonly known as honeycomb toffee because the reaction of the vinegar and bicarbonate of soda with the sugar causes it to froth and set into hundreds of little bubbles that look like honeycomb. In the Dominican Republic and New Zealand it is called Hokey Pokey and you can make New Zealand's popular Hokey Pokey Ice Cream by folding small pieces of cinder toffee into vanilla ice cream.

Makes: about 50 pieces

Preparation time: 10 minutes, plus about 30 minutes setting

Cooking time: 10–15 minutes

Ingredients
unsalted butter, for greasing
450g *(1lb)* granulated sugar
300ml *(10fl oz)* water
4 tbsp malt vinegar
½ tsp bicarbonate of soda

Method

1 Grease an 18cm *(7in)* square baking tin.

2 Put the sugar, water and vinegar into a large, heavy-based saucepan and heat gently, stirring all the time, until the sugar has dissolved.

3 Bring the mixture to the boil, then continue to boil, without stirring, until a little of the mixture, dropped into a cup of cold water, separates into threads that become hard but not brittle. If you are using a sugar thermometer, the toffee should reach 138°C (280°F) (the small crack stage).

4 As soon as threads form, remove the saucepan from the heat and quickly stir in the bicarbonate of soda. Cover your stirring hand with a protective cloth or tea towel because the mixture will bubble fiercely and rise in the pan. As soon the bubbles begin to settle, pour the mixture into the prepared tin. Leave to set.

5 When set, turn the toffee out of the tin and break into pieces. Pack in cellophane bags or between sheets of baking paper in an airtight container. Do not store in the refrigerator or the toffee will become sticky. It will keep in an airtight container for up to a week.

Stuffed dates & figs

Stoned crystallized or dried fruits stuffed with almond paste are always popular, and in this recipe the almond-paste stuffing is homemade. It is easy and quick to prepare but ready-made marzipan can be substituted if time is really short. If you like, the almond paste can be coloured by adding a few drops of edible food colouring and kneading it in well. Red and green are the most traditional colours. Other sorts of dried fruit such as apricots and prunes can also be stuffed.

Makes: about 30 pieces

Preparation time: 15–20 minutes

Cooking time: 5 minutes

Ingredients
55g *(2oz)* icing sugar
85g *(3oz)* caster sugar
115g *(4oz)* ground almonds
1 tsp sherry or brandy (optional)
¼ tsp vanilla extract
½ egg, lightly beaten
125g *(4½oz)* ready-to-eat dried dates
250g *(9oz)* ready-to-eat dried figs
35g *(1¼oz)* blanched almonds

Method

1 Sift the icing sugar into a large bowl. Add 50g *(1¾oz)* of the caster sugar and the ground almonds and mix together well. Add the sherry or brandy, if using, the vanilla extract and enough of the beaten egg to form a stiff paste. Lightly knead the mixture with your hands until smooth.

2 Using a small, sharp knife, carefully slit the dates lengthways without breaking the fruit, and ease out the stones. Cut off the stalks from the figs, slit the fruit and ease gently open.

3 Take small pieces of the almond paste and roll into about 30 small balls, depending upon the number of fruits. Roll the balls into ovals and then place into the centre of the fruits and press together lightly.

4 Preheat the grill. Line the grill pan with a sheet of foil, add the almonds and grill, turning frequently, until toasted on both sides. Remove from the heat.

5 Spread the remaining 35g *(1¼oz)* caster sugar on to a plate and roll the stuffed fruits in the caster sugar to coat them on all sides.

6 Press a toasted almond into the almond paste of each fruit. Place in paper cases and store in an airtight container. The fruits will keep in an airtight container for up to a week.

Chocolate truffles

It is often the truffles in the chocolate box that disappear first, and the homemade variety are especially delicious. If you are making them either for or with children, omit the brandy or rum – they will find it hard to resist eating a few (as will you) as they work. Truffles made with liqueur are best if made a few days before eating to allow the flavour to mellow.

Makes: about 40 truffles

Preparation time: 15–20 minutes, plus 6½–8½ hours cooling/chilling

Cooking time: 5–10 minutes

Ingredients
350g *(12oz)* good-quality dark chocolate (minimum 70% cocoa solids)
115g *(4oz)* unsalted butter, cut into cubes
6 tbsp double cream
2 tbsp brandy or rum (optional)
35g *(1¼oz)* blanched almonds
2 tsp cocoa powder
2 tsp icing sugar

Method

1 Break the chocolate into pieces in a heatproof bowl, then place it over a saucepan of simmering water to melt. Add the butter and cream, and heat together, stirring gently, until all the ingredients have melted and amalgamated.

2 Remove the bowl from the heat. If using, stir in the brandy or rum until smooth. Leave the mixture to cool, cover with clingfilm, then put in the refrigerator for at least 4 hours until the mixture is firm.

3 Line a large baking tray with baking paper. Finely chop the almonds and spread them onto a plate. Spread the cocoa powder onto a second plate, and sift the icing sugar onto a third.

4 Take a heaped teaspoon of the chocolate mixture and, with cold, dampened hands, roll into a ball between your palms. Place on the prepared baking tray and continue until all the mixture has been used.

5 Roll a third of the truffles in the chopped almonds to coat them and return to the baking tray. Coat a third in the cocoa and return to the tray, and then roll the final third in the icing sugar.

6 Cover with clingfilm and chill the truffles in the refrigerator for 2–4 hours until firm. Place in paper or foil sweet cases and store in an airtight container. Homemade truffles should be stored in the refrigerator and are best eaten within two weeks.

Buttered Brazil nuts

These are a real treat for those nostalgic for old-fashioned sweets. Brazil nuts encased in a crunchy butter-toffee coating, for decades a treat on sale – especially at Christmas time – are increasingly difficult to buy, but you can make them at home. They are not difficult, but you need to take care when boiling the hot syrup, and you must work quickly so that the syrup remains liquid. Buttered Brazils are the sweets that most people remember, but walnuts, almonds and macadamias can be given the same delicious treatment.

Makes: about 20 sweets

Preparation time: 15 minutes, plus 1 hour cooling/setting

Cooking time: 20 minutes

Ingredients
50g (1¾oz) unsalted butter, cut into small pieces, plus extra for greasing
60g *(2¼oz)* Brazil nuts
200g *(7oz)* Demerara sugar
2 tsp glucose powder
¼ tsp cream of tartar
6 tbsp water

Method

1 Preheat the oven to 110°C/225°F/Gas Mark ¼. Grease 2 large baking trays and place the Brazil nuts, spaced well apart, on them. Warm in the preheated oven for 5–10 minutes.

2 While the nuts are warming, make the toffee. Put the sugar, remaining butter, glucose powder, cream of tartar and water into a heavy-based saucepan and heat gently, stirring constantly with a wooden spoon, until the sugar has dissolved.

3 Bring the mixture to the boil, then continue to boil, without stirring, until a little of the mixture, dropped into a cup of cold water, separates into threads, which become hard but not brittle. If using a sugar thermometer, the mixture should reach 138°C (280°F) (the small crack stage).

4 As soon as the threads form, remove the pan from the heat, then very quickly spoon small amounts of the toffee mixture over the top of each warmed Brazil nut.

5 Leave until cold. When the buttered Brazils are cold and set, pack between layers of baking paper in an airtight container to store. The nuts should be eaten within two weeks. Do not store them in the refrigerator or they will become sticky.

Rocky Road

This confection of crushed biscuits, nuts and marshmallows, bound together with chocolate, gets its unusual name from its cragged appearance. Rocky Road squares are much loved by children, but you will discover that it is difficult to find an adult who can resist them, too! The ingredients can be varied to suit your taste – for example, you could introduce chopped ready-to-eat apricots, raisins or cranberries instead of the cherries; macadamias, almonds, pistachio nuts or peanuts instead of the Brazil nuts – or even omit the nuts altogether: the make-up of your personal brand of Rocky Road is up to you.

Makes: 16 squares

Preparation time: 15 minutes, plus 3–4 hours cooling/setting

Cooking time: 5–10 minutes

Ingredients

225g *(8oz)* digestive biscuits
75g *(2¾oz)* Brazil nuts
75g *(2¾oz)* glacé cherries
75g *(2¾oz)* mini marshmallows
200g *(7oz)* good-quality dark chocolate
(minimum 80% cocoa solids)
100g *(3½oz)* unsalted butter,
cut into cubes
2 tbsp golden syrup

Method

1 Line an 18cm *(7in)* square, shallow baking tin with baking paper. Put the biscuits in a large, strong polythene bag and crush with a rolling pin until roughly broken up. Roughly chop the nuts and cut the cherries in half. Using kitchen scissors, cut the marshmallows in half.

2 Break the chocolate into pieces in a heatproof bowl and place it over a saucepan of simmering water. Add the butter and golden syrup and heat gently until the chocolate has melted and all the ingredients have amalgamated.

3 Remove the bowl from the heat. Add the crushed biscuits, nuts, cherries and marshmallows and stir together until the ingredients are well mixed and everything is thoroughly coated in the chocolate.

4 Spread the mixture into the prepared tin. Don't press down too hard or smooth it too much – after all, the Road is supposed to be Rocky!

5 Leave for 3–4 hours until cold and set. Cut into squares and store in an airtight container. They should be eaten within two weeks.

Crystallized peel

Crystallized orange and lemon peels are a sophisticated sweet, especially when their ends are dipped in dark chocolate. This recipe uses both oranges and lemons but, if preferred, you can make crystallized peel using just one fruit, or try something more adventurous, such as grapefruit. In addition, without the chocolate and finely chopped, the crystallized peel can be stored in a jar for several months and used as an ingredient in cakes, biscuits, mincemeat, puddings or Chocolate Mendiants (see pages 98–9).

Makes: about 60 pieces

Preparation time: 25–30 minutes, plus 13½–14½ hours cooling/setting/drying

Cooking time: 35–45 minutes

Ingredients

2 thick-skinned oranges
1 large lemon
225g *(8oz)* granulated sugar
225ml *(8fl oz)* water
100g *(3½oz)* caster sugar
85g *(3oz)* good-quality dark chocolate
(minimum 80% cocoa solids)

Method

1 Cut the oranges and lemon in half widthways and then in half again, and use a sharp knife to remove the flesh from the rind. Cut each orange peel into about 6 pieces and each lemon peel into about 5 triangular shapes, about 1cm *(½in)* thick.

2 Put all the peel into a large, heavy-based saucepan, pour in enough cold water to cover and then bring to the boil. Drain, cover with cold water and bring to the boil again. Drain and repeat the procedure three more times. After the last boiling, drain the peel and dry with kitchen paper.

3 Put the granulated sugar and water in a clean saucepan and heat gently, stirring, until the sugar has dissolved. Add the peel, bring to the boil, then boil gently, stirring occasionally, until the syrup has almost evaporated and the peel is transparent. Remove from the heat and leave to cool.

4 Drain the peel well. Spread the caster sugar on a plate and roll each piece of rind in it until coated. Place the peel in a single layer on a wire rack set over a baking sheet. Sprinkle any remaining sugar over the top. Leave to dry for at least 12 hours.

5 To coat the peel in chocolate, line a baking tray with baking paper. Melt the chocolate in a bowl over a pan of simmering water. Remove from the heat.

6 Dip the pieces of peel into the melted chocolate, then place them on the baking tray. Leave for 1–2 hours until set. Pack in an airtight container between sheets of baking paper to store. Do not store in the refrigerator or the peel will become sticky.

Chocolate mendiants

Originally, Mendiants was a fruit and nut dessert from the south of France that was traditionally served on Christmas Eve. It consisted of raisins, figs, hazelnuts and almonds and the colours of each were supposed to resemble the different robes worn by the four orders of mendicant friars – hence the name. Nowadays, Mendiants are thought of as chocolate sweets topped with dried fruits and nuts. You can use whichever fruits and nuts you like best – those in the ingredients list are just there as an example. You can also choose to make the rounds with milk chocolate or even white chocolate: a mixture of different types of chocolate looks particularly attractive.

Method

1 Line several large baking trays with baking paper. Roughly chop the figs. Break the chocolate into pieces in a heatproof bowl, place it over a saucepan of simmering water and heat gently until it has melted.

2 Remove the bowl from the heat and drop heaped teaspoons of melted chocolate onto the prepared baking trays. Use the back of the spoon to spread each mendiant gently into a neat, thin round about 5cm *(2in)* in diameter.

3 Make 3 or 4 mendiants at a time, dotting each round before it sets with an equal quantity of the hazelnuts, almonds, raisins and figs.

4 Leave for 2–3 hours until cold and set. Pack the mendiants carefully between sheets of baking paper in an airtight container to store. They should be eaten within two weeks.

Makes: about 40 chocolates

Preparation time: 20 minutes, plus 2–3 hours cooling/setting

Cooking time: 5–10 minutes

Ingredients
55g *(2oz)* dried figs
200g *(7oz)* good-quality dark chocolate
(minimum 80% cocoa solids)
35g *(1¼oz)* blanched hazelnuts
85g *(3oz)* blanched almonds
50g *(1¾oz)* raisins

Coffee creams

Soft, rich coffee fondant provides a wonderful contrast in texture to the crisp walnut halves that are used to top these sweets. You can either leave them plain, or half-dip them in dark chocolate for a more luxurious finish. Alternatively, you can leave half of them plain and coat the other half in chocolate, as in this recipe. They are particularly good served with an after-dinner cup of espresso coffee.

Makes: about 30 sweets

Preparation time: 20–25 minutes, plus 14½–15½ hours cooling/setting/drying

Cooking time: 5–10 minutes

Ingredients

1½ tsp espresso coffee granules

¾ tsp boiling water

450g *(1lb)* fondant icing sugar, plus extra for dusting

½ tsp cream of tartar

1 tbsp single cream

1 small egg white

75g *(2¾oz)* walnut halves

200g *(7oz)* good-quality dark chocolate (minimum 80% cocoa solids), optional

Method

1 Put the coffee granules in a cup, add the boiling water and stir until dissolved. Set aside and leave to cool.

2 Sift the icing sugar and cream of tartar into a large bowl. Add the cream and the cooled coffee. Lightly whisk the egg white and stir enough into the icing sugar to form a firm, pliable mixture.

3 Turn the fondant onto a clean work surface lightly dusted with icing sugar and knead for 2–3 minutes until smooth. Put it in a polythene bag and leave at room temperature for about 1 hour.

4 Line a baking tray with baking paper. Shape the fondant into balls about 2.5cm *(1in)* in diameter and press a walnut half firmly into the top of each ball. Place on the prepared baking tray and leave in a cool place for about 12 hours until set and completely dry.

5 If using chocolate, break it into pieces in a heatproof bowl, place it over a saucepan of simmering water and heat gently until melted. Remove the bowl from the heat and half-coat half of the coffee creams in the chocolate. Lift out quickly, allowing any excess chocolate to drain against the side of the bowl. Place on the baking tray and leave for 1–2 hours until cold and set. Pack between layers of baking paper in an airtight container to store. The coffee creams should be eaten within two weeks.

Coconut ice

Instantly recognizable by its contrasting block of pastel pink and white, coconut ice is sweet and sticky, and a real treat. This traditional English sweet was usually sold at country fairs and was originally made in slices, but can also be cut into squares and put into sweet cases. It also looks attractive when wrapped in squares of muslin or piled into a cellophane bag or glass jar to give as a gift.

Makes: about 35 pieces

Preparation time: 10–15 minutes, plus about 30 minutes setting

Cooking time: 10–15 minutes

Ingredients

unsalted butter, for greasing
150ml *(5fl oz)* full-fat milk
450g *(1lb)* granulated sugar
125g *(4½oz)* desiccated coconut
2–3 drops red food colouring

Method

1 Grease an 18cm *(7in)* square baking tin. Pour the milk into a large, heavy-based saucepan, stir in the sugar and heat gently, stirring constantly, until the sugar dissolves. Bring to the boil, cover with a lid and boil gently for 2 minutes.

2 Uncover the pan and continue to boil, stirring occasionally, until a little of the mixture, dropped into a cup of cold water, forms into a ball when rolled between the fingers. If using a sugar thermometer, the mixture should reach 116°C (240°F) (the soft ball stage).

3 Remove the pan from the heat and stir in the coconut. Using a wooden spoon, beat the mixture vigorously until it is thick and creamy. Immediately pour half the mixture into the prepared tin and spread it evenly.

4 Dip the end of a skewer into the red food colouring and add a drop or two to the remaining mixture to colour it pink. Add only a tiny drop of colouring at a time – you don't want to overdo it and end up with a lurid red coconut ice. Mix the colour thoroughly into the mixture, then quickly top the white layer in the tin with a second, pink layer and leave to cool until half set.

5 When the mixture is half set, use a sharp knife to mark it into 2.5cm *(1in)* squares. When cold and firm, cut neatly into squares as marked. Pack between layers of baking paper in an airtight container to store. The coconut ice should be eaten within two weeks.

Make a neat lidded box

This box is made from a single sheet of card, and has a narrow, slide-on sleeve to hold it closed – which you can also use to write a greeting or the recipient's name. As with the other boxes, you can either make the sleeve in a contrasting colour or match it to the box.

You will need

1 sheet heavy coloured card, about 300gsm weight, measuring about 50 x 50cm *(20 x 20in)*
craft knife
cutting board
pencil
ruler
1 strip heavy paper (this can be plain, coloured or textured), measuring 50 x 10cm *(20 x 4in)*
scissors
glue
greaseproof paper or tissue

Method

1 Enlarge or photocopy the templates to scale – the finished box will be about 18cm *(7in)* high.

2 Cut the templates out for the box and sleeve, then cut the box out of the heavy card, drawing around the edges with a pencil and ruler. Then cut out the strip of heavy paper you will be using for the sleeve.

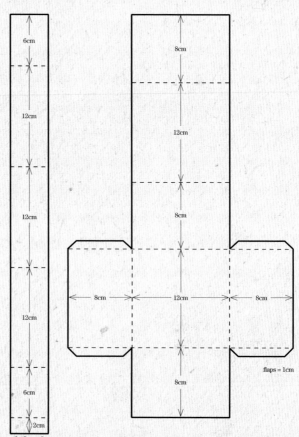

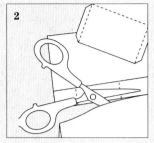

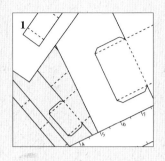

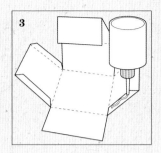

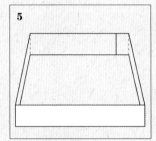

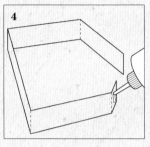

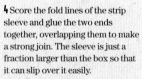

3 Fold the base of the box up and score along the flaps with one blade of a pair of scissors. Fold the four flaps inward and glue them to the inner sides of the box so that you have a base. Leave the glue to dry, then score along the dotted lines to make the lid and the tuck-in flap.

4 Score the fold lines of the strip sleeve and glue the two ends together, overlapping them to make a strong join. The sleeve is just a fraction larger than the box so that it can slip over it easily.

5 Line the box with greaseproof paper or tissue, then fill it with your chosen sweets and fold down the lid. Slide the sleeve over the box. Write a greeting and a note of what's inside on the strip around the side of the box.

Make traditional sweetie bags

With a little folding and gluing you can make sweet bags that look just like the ones old-fashioned sweet shops use – but in a chosen material of your own. Translucent, brightly coloured paper looks good, as does thick art paper with a small window cut into the side to give a glimpse of the contents. You can use pinking shears to cut a zigzag top to the finished bag. Fold it down and hold it in place with a decorative sticker or a sticky label that identifies the sweets inside.

You will need

sheets of thin decorative paper	pencil
craft knife	ruler
cutting board	glue
	scissors

Method

1 Enlarge or photocopy the template to scale – the bag will be 15cm *(6in)* high.

2 Use the template to cut the bag out of the decorative paper. Lightly mark the dotted lines on the wrong side of the paper with a pencil and ruler.

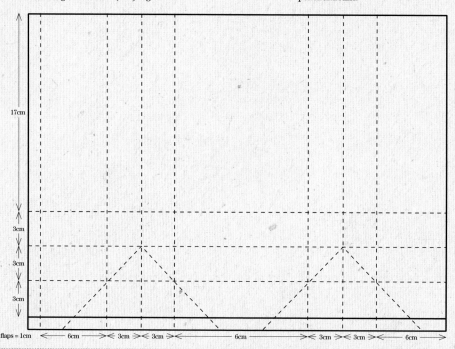

17cm

3cm

3cm

3cm

flaps = 1cm ⟨—— 6cm ——⟩⟨— 3cm —⟩⟨— 3cm —⟩⟨—— 6cm ——⟩⟨— 3cm —⟩⟨— 3cm —⟩⟨—— 6cm ——⟩

3 Make a concertina fold along the three dotted lines of the inner panels, then fold them into a triangular shape as shown in 3. Take one side of the bag and fold along all the vertical lines into a concertina shape (3a). Then fold and reopen all the dotted lines at the base of the bag (this makes it easy to fold the base after the sides are glued).

4 Glue the two open edges together, lapping one over the other. Leave to dry. Now make the base of the bag, folding the end pieces in as shown in 4a and 4b.

5 You should now have two triangular flaps. Fold the upper one down (5) and the lower one up (5a), and glue together where they overlap. Stand the bag upright and leave to dry.

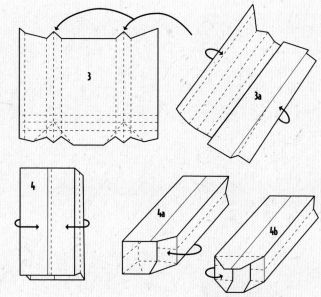

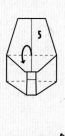

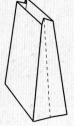

SWEETS & CHOCOLATES

Make a sleeved chocolate box

This carton is made like a box of matches, with a decorative outer sleeve. You can ornament this in any way that you like, using different layers of punched paper, strips of contrasting decorative paper, or, simplest of all, by using a contrasting colour to the inner box. The circle on the box template is an optional cut window – you can fill this with clear film so that the recipient can see what is inside.

You will need

2 sheets of card, measuring at least 25cm x 50cm *(10 x 20in)*. The colours can match or contrast, but both sheets should be at least 300gsm weight in order to make a substantial box
craft knife

scissors
glue
small piece of clear acetate for window, if required
greaseproof paper

Method

1 Enlarge or photocopy the template shown to scale – the finished 'matchbox' will be around 20cm *(8in)* long.

2 Use the template on the card to cut out both the tray and the sleeve of the box. If you want the sleeve to have a window, cut the circle out carefully, keeping the edges smooth.

3 Make up the tray first. Using one blade of a pair of scissors, score along all the dotted lines, then fold the innermost lines so that the sides of the box stand up. Fold the corner tabs in and glue them to the inner sides of the tray. Then fold the outer sections of the box edges in and glue in place to make a substantial tray.

4 If you have cut a window in your box sleeve, glue a square of acetate film on the inner side. When the glue has dried, fold along the dotted lines of the sleeve and glue the edge of one of the outer tabs before laying the other over it. It should slide neatly over the tray.

5 Line the tray with greaseproof paper before filling.

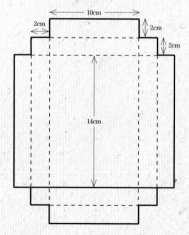

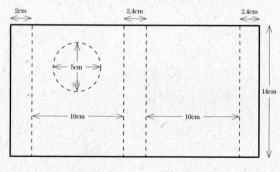

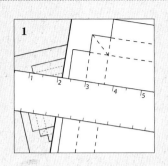

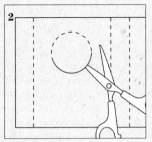

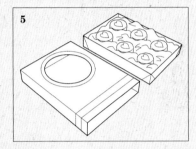

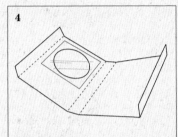

Homemade Drinks & Accompaniments

Whether you want to make a luxurious liqueur, a sparkling spritzer or even a combined food-and-drink treat such as preserved fruits in brandy, a present in a bottle is always well received. This chapter is divided between alcoholic and non-alcoholic drinks (plus a few non-drinking recipes and sauces that will still be presented in their bottles and jars), some of them even using home-harvested flavourings such as elderflowers – so that you will truly be able to say that you collected your ingredients from a nearby hedgerow! From light summer refreshers to winter-warming liqueurs, you'll find something here to suit any seasonal occasion.

Limoncello

In Italy, limoncello is drunk as both an aperitif and a digestif – that is, it may be taken either before or after a meal. Its lemony aroma is particularly delicious when you're sitting outside on a summer's evening. This is one of those presents that is easy to make in quantity and then keep so that you have a present ready when you need one. It will keep for a year. You can store it in a cupboard or in the refrigerator. Limoncello can also be kept in the freezer; it is best drunk very cold and the high spirit content means it doesn't freeze solid and burst the bottles. The raspberry version is a little more unusual, but just as good.

Makes: two 750ml *(1¼ pint)* bottles

Preparation time: 10 minutes, plus 10 days infusing

Cooking time: 20 minutes

Ingredients
5 unwaxed lemons, preferably organic
1 litre *(1¾ pints)* vodka

For the sugar syrup
450g *(1lb)* white granulated sugar
450ml *(16fl oz)* uncarbonated mineral water

Method

1 Use a zester, a swivel-headed vegetable peeler or a small, sharp knife to zest the lemons. If you use the latter, be careful not to remove any of the bitter white pith directly under the peel.

2 Put the zest in a 1 litre *(1¾ pint)* preserving jar and pour in the vodka. Seal the jar and leave for 10 days in a light place, tipping the jar daily to agitate the lemon zest and extract maximum lemon flavour and colour.

3 Then make the sugar syrup. Put the sugar and water into a heavy-based saucepan over a low heat. Bring to the boil, stirring occasionally to ensure the sugar dissolves, then reduce the heat and simmer for 15 minutes. Remove from the heat and leave to cool.

4 Strain the zest from the vodka by pouring it through a fine-meshed sieve directly into the saucepan containing the cooled sugar syrup.

5 Stir well, then decant into clean, sterilized bottles and seal with a cork. Label, and leave to infuse for at least two weeks before drinking.

Variation

To make a raspberry version, omit the lemons and instead add 450g *(1lb)* fresh raspberries to the sugar and water when you are making the sugar syrup. Cook as in step 3, then strain the raspberry syrup through a fine sieve. Add the vodka when the syrup has cooled and leave to infuse for two weeks. This is particularly delicious decanted with sparkling water.

Old-fashioned lemonade

Simultaneously sharp and sweet, homemade lemonade is completely different from any of the varieties you can buy. If you're making it as a present, you may want to include the recipe along with the bottles: people who try it often become addicted and may want to make their own.

Method

1 Using a lemon zester or a sharp vegetable peeler, remove the zest from the lemons, being careful not to include the bitter white pith.

2 Cut the lemons in half and squeeze the juice into a measuring jug, removing any pips as you go. You need to make 450ml *(16fl oz)* of juice.

3 Bring the water to the boil in a saucepan or kettle. Place the sugar and lemon zest in a large, heatproof bowl or saucepan, then pour over the boiling water and stir until the sugar has dissolved. Cover the mixture and leave it to cool for 30 minutes.

4 Strain the cooled syrup into a clean bowl, add the lemon juice and stir the mixture thoroughly.

5 Using a clean funnel, pour or ladle the lemonade into bottles, then cork, or screw on the tops, and refrigerate for about 2 hours before drinking. Serve with ice and an extra slice of lemon. This should be drunk soon after making – it makes a great contribution to a picnic – although it will keep in the refrigerator for about a week if you're making it for home consumption.

Makes: four 500ml *(18fl oz)* bottles

Preparation time: 20 minutes, plus 2½ hours cooling/chilling

Cooking time: 5 minutes

Ingredients
9–12 unwaxed lemons, preferably organic, plus lemon slices to serve
1.4 litres *(2½ pints)* water
115g *(4oz)* caster sugar

Tarragon, chilli & spiced vinegars

Flavoured vinegars lend a distinct kick to homemade salad dressings and sauces, and they're also outstandingly straightforward to make. Be patient when leaving the vinegar to take on its herbal flavour – these aren't instant gifts, but they have the advantage of requiring almost no effort on your part. You could make three small bottles of different flavours and present them together, to offer the recipient a range of tastes to try. Once flavoured, these vinegars will keep well for six months.

Tarragon vinegar

Makes: one 500ml *(18fl oz)* bottle

Preparation time: 10 minutes, plus 30 minutes cooling jar and 3 weeks infusing

Cooking time: none required

Ingredients
about 60g *(2¼oz)* fresh tarragon, plus an extra sprig for the final bottling
500ml *(18fl oz)* white wine vinegar

Chilli vinegar

Makes: one 500ml *(18fl oz)* bottle

Preparation time: 10 minutes, plus 30 minutes cooling jar and 3 weeks infusing

Cooking time: 5 minutes

Ingredients
10–15 fresh red chillies
500ml *(18fl oz)* white wine vinegar

Method – Tarragon vinegar

1 Sterilize a 500ml *(18fl oz)* preserving jar with boiling water, then leave it to cool. Lightly bruise the tarragon (you can just crush it a little in your hand), place it in the jar and pour in the vinegar. Tightly seal the jar, then shake it vigorously.

2 Set the jar aside in a cool, dark place for three weeks, giving it an occasional shake.

3 Choose the bottle in which you'll be presenting the vinegar and sterilize it with boiling water. Strain the vinegar into the bottle, then add an extra sprig of tarragon, seal with a tight-fitting stopper and label.

Method – Chilli vinegar

1 Wash the chillies and trim off the stalks. Cut them in half lengthways and remove the seeds. Wash your hands and scrub your nails well afterwards to avoid getting hot chilli juice anywhere near your eyes.

2 Put the vinegar in a small stainless-steel saucepan, bring gently to the boil then add the chillies. As soon as it boils again, remove from the heat.

3 Pour the hot vinegar and chillies into a warm, sterilized 500ml *(18fl oz)* jar and seal tightly. Give it a good shake and place it somewhere warm and preferably light (a greenhouse or sunny window-sill is ideal). Leave it to infuse for three weeks. Shake the jar every now and then.

4 Strain the vinegar through muslin and pour into a sterilized bottle, adding a whole, fresh chilli if you like, then seal it with a well-fitting stopper and label.

Spiced vinegar

Makes: one 500ml *(18fl oz)* bottle

Preparation time: 15 minutes, plus
1 hour cooling and 2 weeks infusing

Cooking time: 10–15 minutes

Ingredients
500ml *(18fl oz)* white wine vinegar
1 tsp coriander seeds
1 tsp whole cloves
1 tsp finely chopped fresh root ginger
1 tsp star anise, broken up into 3 or 4 pieces
1 unwaxed lemon
1 tsp black peppercorns
5 sprigs fresh coriander

Method – Spiced vinegar

1 In a small stainless-steel saucepan,
combine the vinegar, coriander seeds,
cloves, ginger and star anise. Simmer
gently over a low heat for about 10
minutes, being careful not to allow it to
boil. Remove from the heat and leave it
to cool completely.

2 Pour everything into a sterilized 500ml
(18fl oz) jar, seal and leave it for about
two weeks in a cool, dark place. Give it
a shake every so often.

3 Use a zester to remove about a
teaspoonful of zest from the lemon and put
it into a decorative, sterilized bottle. Strain
the vinegar mixture through a fine sieve
or a piece of muslin into a jug, then use a
clean funnel to decant it into the bottle.
Add the peppercorns and fresh coriander,
seal with a well-fitting stopper and label.
It is ready to use immediately.

Flavoured vodkas

Vodka has become much more popular over the last decade, and these fruit-flavoured vodkas are delicious drunk in little shot glasses or used with mixers to make a long, refreshing drink. Since vodka has hardly any flavour of its own, it takes on other tastes particularly well. You do not have to use top-grade vodka for these flavoured varieties: the cheaper supermarket own brands will work well. These recipes feature raspberry, blueberry and grapefruit as flavourings, but almost any citrus or berry fruit will taste good.

Method

1 Put your chosen fruit into a 1 litre *(1¾ pint)* sterilized jar, pour over the vodka and seal. Shake the jar well.

2 Leave the jar in a cool, dark place for about a week. Shake it once a day to help the infusion.

3 After a week, taste the vodka. If you want a stronger fruit flavour, you may need to leave it to infuse for a few more days. When you are happy with the taste, strain the vodka through muslin, or a very fine sieve, into a sterilized 750ml *(1¼ pint)* bottle with a tight-fitting stopper, then label. The vodka is ready to drink as soon as it has been decanted into bottles and will keep well for at least a year.

Makes: one 750ml *(1¼ pint)* bottle

Preparation time: 10 minutes, plus 1–2 weeks infusing

Cooking time: none required

Ingredients

Raspberry vodka
200g *(7oz)* fresh raspberries, with any stalks or leaves removed
750ml *(1¼ pints)* vodka

Blueberry vodka
200g *(7oz)* fresh blueberries, with any stalks or leaves removed
750ml *(1¼ pints)* vodka

Grapefruit vodka
1 large grapefruit, peeled, with as much pith removed as possible, and thinly sliced
750ml *(1¼ pints)* vodka

Sweet syrups

These pomegranate and blueberry syrups taste delicious diluted with mineral water – they make a cheerful alternative to an alcoholic drink for the drivers at a party, and children often enjoy them because they have the requisite sweetness but seem much more sophisticated than everyday juice drinks. They are also good trickled over cream desserts; you could even swirl a couple of spoonfuls through half-frozen homemade ice cream or semifreddo to make fruit 'ripple' flavours.

Pomegranate syrup

Makes: one 450ml *(16fl oz)* bottle

Preparation time: 15 minutes, plus 1 hour cooling and overnight infusing

Cooking time: 5 minutes

Ingredients
2 large pomegranates
granulated sugar, amount equal to the weight of the peeled fruit
juice of 1 lemon

Spiced blueberry syrup

Makes: one 450ml *(16fl oz)* bottle

Preparation time: 10 minutes, plus 15 minutes cooling

Cooking time: 20 minutes

Ingredients
350g *(12oz)* blueberries
juice of 1 lemon
juice of 1 orange
½ tsp allspice
100g *(3½oz)* granulated sugar

Method – Pomegranate syrup

1 Score the skin of the pomegranates into quarters with a knife. Break the fruit along the score lines so that you have eight quarters. Carefully de-seed them, then weigh the skinned seeds.

2 Put the seeds into a lidded container with an equal weight of granulated sugar, then add the lemon juice. Put on the lid and leave the mixture overnight in a cool place.

3 The next day, empty the mixture into a saucepan, bring to the boil, then reduce the heat and simmer gently for 2 minutes.

4 Leave the syrup to cool, then strain it into a bowl through muslin, squeezing to extract all the juice.

5 Pour the syrup into a sterilized bottle, then seal and label. When cold, store in the refrigerator. You can use it straight away, and it will keep for four weeks in the refrigerator. It also freezes well.

Method – Spiced blueberry syrup

1 Put all the ingredients into a saucepan and bring the mixture slowly to the boil over a medium heat. Stir occasionally.

2 When the mixture has boiled, reduce the heat and simmer gently for about 15 minutes until thick and syrupy.

3 Remove from the heat and leave to cool slightly, then strain through muslin, giving it a squeeze to extract all the juice.

4 Use a funnel to decant the syrup into a 450ml *(16fl oz)* warm, sterilized bottle, then seal and label. Leave until it is completely cold before refrigerating.

Dessert sauces

Most puddings are improved by a spoonful of hot fudge or white chocolate sauce, and these homemade versions are particularly good. Opinion is divided on whether the white or the dark version is better – make large batches of both and give your recipients a jar of each so that they can decide for themselves. These sauces set quite solid in the jar, so they should be spooned into a small saucepan and warmed gently before serving. They don't keep for more than three weeks in the refrigerator (although they can be frozen successfully), but they will usually be eaten up long before their deadline, so this is unlikely to prove a problem.

Method – Hot fudge sauce

1 Put the butter and the cocoa powder into a small saucepan and slowly melt together over a gentle heat.

2 Stir the water, sugar and golden syrup into the cocoa and butter mixture. Bring it all to a rolling boil, reduce the heat and simmer for 3 minutes.

3 Pour the sauce immediately into a 225g *(8oz)* warm, sterilized jar, then seal and label. Leave it to cool completely, then store in the refrigerator.

Method – White chocolate sauce

1 Cut the butter into small cubes and melt it in a heatproof bowl set over a saucepan of simmering water.

2 Chop the chocolate into chunks and add it to the melted butter, a few pieces at a time, stirring constantly until the mixture has melted and amalgamated.

3 Stir the cream into the butter and chocolate mixture until all the ingredients have melted together into a smooth sauce.

4 Pour the sauce immediately into a 225g *(8oz)* warm, sterilized jar, then seal and label. Leave to cool completely before storing in the refrigerator.

Hot fudge sauce

Makes: one 225g *(8oz)* jar

Preparation time: 5–10 minutes, plus 1 hour cooling

Cooking time: 5–10 minutes

Ingredients
60g *(2¼oz)* butter
6 tbsp good-quality cocoa powder
5 tbsp water
175g *(6oz)* granulated sugar
2 tbsp golden syrup

White chocolate sauce

Makes: one 225g *(8oz)* jar

Preparation time: 5–10 minutes, plus 1 hour cooling

Cooking time: 5–10 minutes

Ingredients
70g *(2½oz)* unsalted butter
300g *(10½oz)* good-quality white chocolate
150ml *(5fl oz)* double cream

Clementines in brandy

Fruit marries with brandy very well, and clementines in brandy not only look extremely festive but are also a great treat both to eat and to drink. You can drain off the warm, orange-scented brandy to drink in small shot glasses, and cut the fruit into small segments to eat with pouring cream, or alongside ice cream. Take care when you are arranging the clementines in their jar; pack them in quite closely and face the tops of the fruit outwards to make this an attractive present visually, as well as appealing to eat.

Makes: one 750ml *(1¼ pint)* jar

Preparation time: 15 minutes, plus 1 hour cooling

Cooking time: 5 minutes

Ingredients

12 clementines

7 whole cloves

4 tbsp mineral water

100g *(3½oz)* caster sugar

600ml *(1 pint)* brandy

Method

1 Sterilize a 750ml *(1¼ pint)* preserving jar with boiling water, empty it, then leave it to cool.

2 Peel the clementines (save the peel of one of them to use later) and, using a sharp knife, strip away as much of the white pith as possible. It is worth spending some time on this because it will make the end result look much more polished.

3 Carefully pack the clementines in the preserving jar, arranging them attractively. Put a clove into the centre of each of the top three clementines, so that they look neat when the jar is first opened.

4 Put the water, sugar, remaining 4 cloves and the reserved peel into a heavy-based saucepan and heat gently until the sugar dissolves. Simmer for 2 minutes.

5 Remove the syrup from the heat, strain it carefully through a sieve and leave to cool completely. When it is cold, pour in the brandy.

6 Pour the syrup and brandy mixture over the clementines, covering them completely, then seal the jar and label. Store in a cool, dark place and eat within three months.

Elderflower cordial

The light, flowery taste of elderflower cordial is one of the most refreshing and individual flavours, quite unlike anything else. The fragrance of this drink transports you instantly to the long days of early summer, when the hedgerows are full of the lacy, flowering heads. And, since the cordial easily lasts for a year, this really is a taste of summer that you can enjoy well into the winter months. You need to gather the flower heads yourself, though – they are not for sale.

Makes: four 750ml *(1¼ pint)* bottles

Preparation time:
30 minutes, plus 5 days infusing

Cooking time: 5 minutes

Ingredients
20 elderflower heads
1.5 litres *(2¾ pints)* water
1.8 kg *(4lb)* granulated sugar
70 g *(2½oz)* citric acid (you can buy
this at the chemist)
½ campden tablet (from a wine/beer
making shop), crushed
slices of fresh lemon

Method

1 First find your hedgerow! Choose a warm, sunny day (it's better if the flower heads aren't too wet), then pick 20 large elderflower heads. Inspect them for insects and give them a gentle shake before placing in a basket or bag.

2 Rinse the elderflowers briefly under a cold running tap, then shake off any surplus water. Boil the 1.5 litres *(2¾ pints)* of water in a large saucepan, then remove from the heat and add the sugar, citric acid and elderflowers. Stir to dissolve the sugar, then cover the pan with a lid and leave to stand in a cool place for five days, stirring twice daily.

3 Strain the liquid through muslin into a large bowl, crush half a campden tablet with the back of a spoon, and stir it into the cordial. The campden tablet will help it to last well.

4 Pour the cordial into four 750ml *(1¼ pint)* clean, sterilized bottles, seal them with tight-fitting tops, then label. The cordial is ready to use straight away – just dilute it to taste with water and add ice and a slice of lemon. The bottles will last up to a year. Store them in a cool, dark place such as a larder or cupboard.

Sloe gin

It is unusual for a homemade liqueur recipe to feature gin as a base, rather than vodka or brandy – but sloe gin is exactly what it says. The sloe is the fruit of the blackthorn bush, and doesn't have many applications other than its appearance in this subtle herbal drink. It has a very distinctive flavour, which enthusiasts prefer to all other liqueurs. Sloes can be seen in the hedgerows in autumn and traditionalists say that you should gather them and make your gin only in November after the first frost, which is alleged to give the drink more flavour.

Makes: two 750ml *(1¼ pint)* bottles

Preparation time: 30 minutes, plus 24 hours freezing and 3 weeks maturing

Cooking time: none required

Ingredients
sufficient sloes to half-fill two
750ml *(1¼ pint)* bottles
175g *(6oz)* granulated sugar
1 litre *(1¾ pint)* bottle of gin

Method

1 Pick the sloes when they have fully ripened (they are ripe when the skin has a slight bloom on it). Wash them thoroughly, picking out any leaves or detritus. Take a darning needle and prick each sloe two or three times, then half-fill two 750ml *(1¼ pint)* sterilized bottles with sloes. Put the bottles into the freezer for 24 hours. This ensures that the sloes have their 'first frost', which is believed to sweeten them and to help them release their flavour into the gin.

2 Take the bottles out of the freezer and, using a funnel, pour half of the granulated sugar into each bottle.

3 Fill both bottles up with gin, put the lids on and shake them well.

4 Leave the gin to mature for at least three weeks. Shake the bottles well at least once a day.

5 If you are giving the gin as a present, after three weeks you can decant it into clean bottles. Leaving the sloes in won't harm the taste, but the clear, red liquid looks very pretty on its own. The gin can be drunk after the initial maturing period and will last for up to two years.

Crème de cassis

A traditional French vodka-based liqueur, crème de cassis is usually served diluted with white wine or mineral water. It is rich and fruity; blackcurrants give it a very identifiable and individual taste (a newer drink made in the same way but with blackberries – crème de mures – is a variation that you could also try if you have a late-summer glut of soft fruit. Use red wine of a reasonable quality to make your cassis; cheap or sour wine will affect the smoothness of the finished liqueur. This recipe takes a little time and effort, so you might like to double the quantities to give you a stock of cassis – both as presents, and to drink yourself.

Makes: two 750ml *(1¼ pint)* bottles

Preparation time: 30 minutes, plus 48 hours infusing

Cooking time: 2 hours

Ingredients

1kg *(2lb 4 oz)* blackcurrants, washed

1 litre *(1¾ pints)* good red wine

granulated sugar (for quantity, see method)

900ml *(1½ pints)* vodka

Method

1 Place the blackcurrants in a large bowl and pour over the wine. Cover the bowl with a tea towel, set aside in a cool place and leave it for 48 hours.

2 Take another large bowl and spread a large piece of muslin over it. Feed the soaked blackcurrants into a food processor in batches and empty the pulp into the muslin-covered bowl. Gather the corners of the muslin together, lift it up and squeeze out as much juice as you can.

3 Measure out the blackcurrant juice, pour it into a preserving pan and, for each litre of juice, add 1kg *(2lb 4 oz)* of granulated sugar. Gently heat to dissolve the sugar, stirring constantly.

4 Using a thermometer to regulate the temperature, keep the mixture over a gentle heat for about 2 hours, but do not allow it to simmer – your aim should be to keep it tepid, at about blood temperature. You will need to check it after the first 15 minutes and then every half hour or so. Give the syrup a thorough stir whenever you check. After 2 hours, remove it from the heat and leave it to cool.

5 Take a teacup and a large bowl and measure 3 cupfuls of syrup into the bowl, followed by one cup of vodka. Repeat, continuing with the 3:1 ratio until all the syrup is used up. Stir the mixture well.

6 Use a funnel to pour your cassis into clean, sterilized bottles, then seal them with tight-fitting corks or screw-on tops, and label. The cassis will be ready to drink after three more days, and will keep well for a year.

Coffee liqueur

If you know someone who is not keen on very sweet and fruity liqueurs, this strong, rich coffee concoction may be more to his or her taste. The mixed rum-and-vodka base gives it a depth and warmth that makes it seem more appropriate as a winter drink, although it can also be good accompanying an espresso and served in a shot glass with a couple of lumps of ice on a hot evening. You do need to use proper, strong espresso coffee to give it a very authentic flavour.

Method

1 Make a fresh brew of espresso coffee. Measure out 225ml *(8fl oz)* of the hot coffee, pour it into a bowl, then add the sugar and stir until it has completely dissolved. Leave to cool.

2 When the sweetened coffee is completely cold, pour it into a sterilized preserving jar and add the two spirits. Cut the vanilla pod in half lengthways and add it to the jar, then put on the lid and leave it in a cool, dark place, such as a larder or storecupboard, for four weeks.

3 After four weeks, strain the liqueur through muslin into a saucepan, use a funnel to pour it into a clean, sterilized 750ml *(1¼ pint)* bottle, then seal with a tight-fitting lid and label. The liqueur will keep well for up to a year.

Makes: one 750ml *(1¼ pint)* bottle

Preparation time: 10–15 minutes, plus 4 weeks infusing

Cooking time: 5 minutes

Ingredients
225ml *(8fl oz)* espresso coffee
225g *(8oz)* granulated sugar
225ml *(8fl oz)* vodka
225ml *(8fl oz)* rum
1 vanilla pod

Winter liqueur

There is something truly festive about this liqueur's blend of spices – warm and exotic, it makes a good Christmas present. Again, a mixed base – vodka and brandy in this case – adds a depth to its flavour. If you are serving it during festive occasions, it goes very well with sweet things, complementing a slice of Christmas cake or gingerbread. If you are feeling really generous you could give a bottle as a gift, accompanied by the dark, cherry-topped fruit cake on pages 44–5.

Method

1 Sterilize a large preserving jar with boiling water, then empty it. When it is cool, put in all the spices, then pour in the vodka and the brandy. Seal the jar and leave in a cool, dark place for two weeks.

2 Strain the liqueur through a double layer of muslin into a large bowl.

3 Put the sugar into a small saucepan and add the water. Warm gently over a low heat until the sugar has dissolved. Leave to cool.

4 Measure 225ml *(8fl oz)* of the cooled syrup and add this to the spiced alcohol.

5 Use a funnel to decant the liqueur into a clean, sterilized 750ml *(1¼ pint)* bottle. It will be ready to drink after a week, and will keep for up to a year.

Makes: one 750ml *(1¼ pint)* bottle

Preparation time: 30 minutes, plus 2 weeks infusing

Cooking time: 5 minutes

Ingredients
2 cinnamon sticks
4 whole cloves
1 tsp allspice berries
1 tsp ground coriander
2 star anise
550ml *(19fl oz)* vodka
225ml *(8fl oz)* brandy
225g *(8oz)* granulated sugar
125ml *(4fl oz)* water

Labelled sleeves for homemade bottles

You can add a more professional look to your homemade liqueurs by making sleeves to slip round them. They can be as plain or as decorative as you like – they are simply made from strips of medium-weight paper, with the patterns photocopied or traced on. You can add colour or leave them plain, and the pattern can be simple, like these basic floral examples, or more complex.

You will need

tape measure
medium-weight photocopy paper
coloured pencils (optional)
scissors
double-sided tape

Method

1 Measure your bottle around the centre, and add 2.5cm *(1in)* extra for the sleeve to overlap. Take a sheet of paper at least as long as the bottle's circumference and the overlap allowance. Photocopy a pattern shown here onto the paper, or choose your own. Use coloured pencils to add colour (if required).

2 Cut out the pattern strip and wrap it around the bottle. Fasten the overlap neatly with 1–2 small tags of double-sided tape.

Labels for your creations

A customized label looks much better than just the standard sticky sort, and these designs can be scanned or colour-photocopied to add polish to your jams, jellies and bottled treats. You can buy label paper with a peel-off backing for your printer. Then just add a name and the date the treat was made, and it's ready for use.

If you enjoy drawing, you can copy the designs here in freehand, or invent some of your own. Don't forget that simple ideas usually work better than elaborate ones, and even a plain label framed with a single coloured line drawn around the outer edge can look very effective contrasted against the beautiful, clear colour of a jelly or a liqueur.

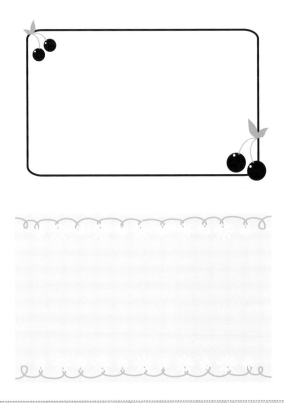

Index

Acknowledgements

The publisher would like to thank the following for providing props for photography:

Adamczewski, 196 High Street, Lewes BN7 2NS

Bright Ideas, 38 High Street, Lewes BN7 2LU

Monsieur Canelle et Compagnon, The Old Needlemakers, West Street, Lewes BN7 2NZ

Pen to Paper, 170a High Street, Lewes BN7 1YE

Revive-all, The Old Needlemakers, West Street, Lewes BN7 2NZ

Steamer Trading, 20/21 High Street, Lewes BN7 2BY